FROM THIS FAITH FORWARD

COMPILED BY JOYCE WILLIAMS

Beacon Hill Press of Kansas City
Kansas City, Missouri

Copyright 2005
by Joyce Williams and Beacon Hill Press of Kansas City

ISBN 083-412-1867

Printed in the
United States of America

Cover Design: Royce Ratcliff
Cover Photo: Stockbyte Photography

Library of Congress Cataloging-in-Publication Data

From this faith forward / compiled by Joyce Williams.
   p. cm.
  ISBN 0-8341-2186-7 (pbk.)
  1. Christian women—Religious life. I. Williams, Joyce, 1944-

  BV4527.F76 2005
  248.8'43—dc22

2005009742

10 9 8 7 6 5 4 3 2 1

CONTENTS

FOREWORD

The world is fascinated with famous people, and the church is no different. Our heroes are usually wonderful Christians who have turned their pieces of the world upside down. Joyce Williams has gathered stories of well-known Christians and filled out their lives a little for us.

I don't know about you, but I want to hang around the people who know how to love God, serve God in their own spheres, whether sacred or secular, and bring glory to God as they live their lives—often under a microscope. But how do you and I hang around famous people? They're difficult to get close to! They often have entourages, even in the Christian world. I'll tell you a secret. You can hang around them in a book! Get to know their secrets of spiritual intimacy with God, their secrets of prayer and effectiveness.

As we look through the window of their faith, we will be encouraged to believe the ground is level at the foot of the cross. Our sisters who are given the limelight would be the first to agree they are very ordinary people with an extraordinary God living inside of them. They have learned to yield their lives to His control, believing that He never calls without equipping, whatever the task. That is something we can all do. I recommend these stories and pray they encourage you in your walk with Him.

Jill Briscoe

ACKNOWLEDGMENTS

This book would not have been written without the encouragement of my husband, Gene. He continues to be president of my fan club (and I hold the same office for him!). Also, thanks to Beacon Hill Press of Kansas City for believing in me.

There's no way to thank all who have invested in my life by sharing their faith with me—my parents, family, pastors and their wives, teachers, friends—the list is enormous. I'm grateful to each one. I plan to thank each of you personally when we meet in heaven.

In recent months I've been especially touched and blessed by the witness and example of Carole and Roger Costa. Carole and Roger, I want to specifically tell you how deeply I appreciate your sharing, tender, helpful spirits. You embody the love of Christ as you give of yourselves unstintingly with no expectation of return. From orphanages in Bulgaria to prison ministry to using your home as a safe haven, your lovingkindness is evident to all. Thank you for being Christ's channels of love.

My prayer is that you, the reader, will be encouraged and challenged to be strong and bold in sharing your faith as you read these stories of courageous, godly women from around the world. May you and I leave a faith-filled legacy for those who come after us.

1

LORI
BECKLER

One Friday afternoon in December, as I sat at my computer, a thought came to me: *Why not start a women's Promise Keepers-style conference?* I was very busy at work, so I didn't pay too much attention to it. But when I caught myself thinking about it again later, I began to get excited.

My husband, Bob, was away coaching a high school basketball game that I would also be attending later in the day, but I couldn't call him right then. When I arrived at the game I knew better than to interrupt him while he was coaching. I could hardly contain my excitement. However, God knew how to get Bob's attention. During a time out, He brought the same thought to him. Intriguingly, God interrupted each of us so that we would know the voice was His!

God uses our experiences and our gifts to further His purposes. He used my background in travel and convention planning and my heart for women, and He blended that with Bob's passion for evangelism and his heart for families. We agreed that God had planted these thoughts, so we began to pray and brainstorm.

As we shared together, we wondered, *How many should we plan for—200 or 2,000? Whom should we invite to speak and do the music?* I remember thinking, *Lord, you sure haven't written this all down on my checklist, so I'm not sure how to plan for something without more details and direction.* But since we were totally surrendered to God, it wasn't long before everything started falling into place. It became increasingly clear that it wasn't *our* plan. God was in charge!

Everything seemed to be coming together, but this women's conference needed a name. Our close-knit family was together on a Sunday in Winfield, Kansas. After church, my mother, aunts, cousins, sister, and I sat around the kitchen table sharing about what was going on in each of our lives. Our common bond of faith and love for our Lord and Savior Jesus Christ permeated our conversation. When it was my turn, I told them about God's call on Bob and me to begin a women's conference. I asked them to ask God's blessing and direction for this new ministry and to pray that we would find just the right name.

We got out Grandma's Bible. As we searched the pages,

we agreed that His Word was our holy heritage that had been passed on to us and that we must pass it on to others. As we began to read Ps. 78:4, all of us realized we had hit upon it: "We will tell the next generation the praiseworthy deeds of the LORD." We were so excited. We agreed that we want to be heritage keepers. And that's how Heritage Keepers was born.

The first Heritage Keepers Conference was held in Wichita, Kansas, in 1996. More than 2,000 women from 18 states gathered. Since that time, God has taken our ministry to Oklahoma City, Denver, Indianapolis, and Nashville. Thousands of women's lives have been transformed as they have accepted Jesus Christ as Savior. Many others have rededicated their lives.

Today we feel blessed to have three generations of our extended family and friends serving God through Heritage Keepers. God is allowing us to live out our holy heritage by ministering together for His glory.

As we prepare to celebrate Heritage Keepers' 10th anniversary, we know that God has given us four words He wants us to share through this ministry: *covenant, inheritance, generation,* and *heritage.*

- God's promised *covenant* is our foundation.
- From his covenant comes our promised *inheritance.*
- Our mission is to pass it to the next *generation.*
- And our goal is to leave a godly *heritage.*

Once again, we step out in faith, trusting Him in all things and obeying His leading and direction. God is calling us to help each woman embrace her holy legacy and then to pass it on to the next generation—to be heritage keepers of our faith.

2

RINA
BISWAS

*S*akina trembled with fear as she huddled on the dark street corner. She was barely 13 years old and had just finished the sixth grade. Her stepmother did not like the fact that Sakina was maturing, so that morning she had thrown Sakina out of their tiny hovel with only the clothes on her back and told her never to return. As she roamed the streets that day, she had no idea where she would spend the night. Then a woman grabbed her and forced her to a brothel, promising food and shelter in return for giving herself to men. She told Sakina, "If you don't sell your body and give the money to me, I'll kill you." At sunset she dragged her to a busy intersection.

A man approached Sakina, roughly pushed her into a filthy alcove, and raped her. When she began to scream in pain, he beat her until she was silent. Then he threw a few rupees on her bleeding body, kicked her one more time, and left.

Clutching her torn clothing around her, Sakina slowly rose to her feet. The woman had been watching from the shadows, and she quickly darted across the street and grabbed the money. She slapped Sakina and told her to stop whimpering. Then she roughly pulled Sakina up and shoved her back to the street corner. Sakina lost count of the number of men who used her before sunrise. Finally, she was allowed to return to a tiny corner in the brothel, where she spent the day racked with pain and aching with disgrace. This became the pattern of her life.

Early one morning months later, Sakina limped back in the direction of the brothel. Pastor Sukamal Biswas and his wife, Rina, a public health nurse, came to her on the street. They visited the red light district regularly to rescue abandoned young girls who had been forced into prostitution. Gently, Rina pushed back Sakina's matted hair and told her that they wanted to help. Sakina recognized that there was something different about them and that they really cared. Quickly, they ran around the corner so that no one from the brothel could see them.

They accompanied Sakina to the police station to report the illegal sex trade. Then they took her to their home and filled a tub with warm water so that she could bathe her battered body. As she gobbled the rice and chicken they put before her, Rina heard about Jesus for the first time in her life. She could see His love in their caring faces. Sakina slept through the night until almost noon the next day. For the first time in months, she felt safe.

Pastor and Rina Sukamal, along with the church they pastor, partner with CARE International. They work with Project Shakti, a ministry designed to help prostitutes break free from life on the streets. God has called them to rescue these girls and show them that there's hope as they lead them to Jesus and mentor them in their new faith. The day after they rescued Sakina, they took her to a rehabilitation center that provides for the care and recovery of young prostitutes. Rina tenderly embraced Sakina and gave her tracts to read so that she could come to know Jesus.

That night as Sakina lay down on a tiny cot, she clutched the tracts and prayed to Jesus, the Biswases' God. She wanted to experience the peace and love they had demonstrated.

Sakina is at great risk for the HIV virus, and she has not yet been tested. But she is comforted to know that the pathway of her life has been changed for eternity.

3

CAROLINE BRUCE

It was a wonderful experience to represent the United States at the 2004 Olympics in Athens, and it was a joy to have such a platform for sharing my faith in Jesus Christ. My goals throughout competition were to meet as many people as possible, find ways to glorify God, and share my faith while being a godly ambassador for my country.

My strong, supportive extended family members are great encouragers in the faith, leading me to accept Christ at an early age. Because of that foundation of faith, I kept repeating Jeremy Camp's song "I Will Trust in You" while competing. I know that my talent is a gift from God and that swimming is a platform for telling others about my faith.

I've learned that it's better to be loved for being God's ambassador than for my athletic talent. God gives us the freedom to be our best. The Olympic experience is simply another stepping stone in my life that's fulfilled by my faith in Jesus.

4

GRACIA
BURNHAM

I was patient for about ten weeks, waiting on God for Martin and me to be rescued following our capture by terrorists in the Philippines. Day after day, week after week, month after month, our hopes soared when word came that the ransom was going to be paid and we would be released. Time after time, however, our hopes were dashed.

Ten weeks into our captivity, I had a crisis of faith; I was depressed, and I was angry with God. One day as I anguished on a riverbank, I knew that I had to decide whether I was going to continue harboring my dark feelings and sinking deeper into despair or if I was going to believe God and His promises.

There's no doubt that Martin and I were in extreme crisis—captives in the jungles of the Philippines. I felt God was far away, and He seemed to be ignoring our pleas. But I realized that I must cling to my faith. In that moment, God all but audibly spoke to me and said, *If you believe that I died for you, can't you believe that I still love you?*

His peace and assurance swept over me like the waters of the swiftly moving river. I felt enveloped in His love. Even though danger surrounded us every moment of the day and our future was uncertain, I thanked God for giving me an oasis of peace.

In the tortuous months that followed I was grateful for that faith lift in the jungle of despair.

5

LAURA
BUSH

*L*aura Bush emanates serenity and peace as she meets the challenges she faces each day as first lady, wife of United States President George W. Bush. We're blessed to have a first lady who speaks openly about the faith she and her husband share. The following is excerpted from her remarks at the New York Tenth Anniversary Prayer Breakfast in May 2004 and reflects the strength and courage that exemplify her faith in God.

Today, we celebrate the vital role of faith in our lives and in our nation. We give thanks to God for the blessings bestowed on us. We seek forgiveness for our sins and renewal for our souls.

Today, we gather not as people of many faiths, but as a fellowship of faithful who share in a love of God and humanity. We pray to find meaning and purpose in our lives. For in prayer, we recognize that we are loved and called to love, and that we can give hope and be hopeful.

Millions of Americans seek guidance every day in prayer. I'm one of them. I also know that many Americans remember President Bush and me in their prayers, and we are grateful. I'm blessed to be married to a man who is strong enough to bear great burdens and humble enough to ask God for help. We draw on our faith in times of joy and also in times of uncertainty. This was especially true in the days after September 11th.

On the Sunday after those attacks, the President and I attended church at Camp David. Remarkably, the psalm outlined in the lectionary for that September Sunday was Psalm 27.

It reads, "Thy face, LORD, will I seek. . . [I believe that I shall] see the goodness of the LORD in the land of the living" [KJV]. Given the week's tragic events, the words carried enormous meaning—because that's exactly what we saw.

We witnessed a handful of people commit an unbelievable atrocity, but we saw millions more commit acts of care and compassion. Because of this, I chose Psalm 27 for our first White House holiday card. This was a small way to pay tribute to the resiliency and the goodness of the American people.

As a nation, we've grown stronger since that day and also more generous. Since that day Americans have offered many prayers. And we continue to pray for the strength of our nation. We pray for those who lost their lives on September 11th and for those who still live with the tragedy of that day.

We pray for our military men and women who defend our lives with their own and for their families who sacrifice so much. We pray for those who've fallen in service to our country and for their loved ones, that they may find comfort and strength. And we pray for the people of Iraq and Afghanistan, that they may live in peace and freedom.

We have many reasons to pray, and every reason to believe that God listens to our prayers. Life itself is our greatest blessing. Our faith and our families are extraordinary gifts.

And we're blessed to live in a nation that upholds the freedom to worship as a God-given right. The psalm you have chosen as your theme today, "Blessed is the nation whose God is the Lord," speaks to our faith in God and in each other.

For me, this psalm means that our nation is blessed because we have people of faith performing acts of faith. Those who believe in a higher power believe that we all have a higher calling.

My husband often says that government can provide resources, but it can't put hope in our hearts or a sense of purpose in our lives. In solving the problems of our day, there is no substitute for love and personal contact. As a people of faith, we know that much is required of us. And many Americans, like Julio Medina, believe that faith can make a difference in our lives and in our communities.

I invited Julio, a New Yorker, to sit with me during the President's last State of the Union Address. Julio was born and raised in the South Bronx. Julio's mother worked long hours in a factory so she could send her seven children to Catholic school. His family was very close, but they struggled to get by. When he was 13, he decided to help out by selling drugs.

His efforts to help turned into years of drug abuse and crime and more than a decade in prison. But Julio found something behind the prison walls. He earned a bachelor's degree from State University of New York and his master's from the New York Theological Seminary. He'd always believed in God, but in prison he found the strength to believe in himself.

Julio said the turning point came when his niece came to visit him. She was excited to introduce her boyfriend. She said Julio would like him because they were similar. Julio found out that what they had in common was drugs.

Julio was determined to erase the image that his family had of him. When he was released, he remembered the lessons he had learned and the faith he had found.

He experienced firsthand the effects of social prejudice against former prison inmates, so he started the Exodus Transitional Community to help prisoners transition into society. At Exodus, Julio helps former prisoners write résumés, find jobs, learn computer skills, and find housing. And they begin every day in prayer.

Julio said, "We give thanks for the blessings we have and we ask God to help us meet the struggles of the day."

This is the power of prayer—and the liberating freedom of faith. Julio reminds us that when we share hope and healing with others, we make America a more hopeful place for all.

God has blessed our nation and our lives beyond measure. And today we pray that God will grant us the courage and the conviction to celebrate our faith, to serve others, and to seek comfort in prayer. This is our prayer for all nations and for all of God's people.

From the White House web site: <www.whitehouse.gov>

6
MARGE
CALDWELL

arge Caldwell has been a mentor to thousands over the years. The impact she has made upon eternity is yet to be known.

Beth Moore is one of the greatest Bible study teachers and communicators of all times; millions around the world participate in her Bible studies. To a great extent, each person who has taken part in one of Beth's studies is a reflection of Marge Caldwell's influence. In her dedication to Marge in her book *Jesus, the One and Only*, Beth Moore writes,

To Marge Caldwell, my mother and teacher in ministry . . .

You were the first person whose passionate love for Jesus took my breath away. I will never comprehend how I have been so blessed by God to know you, love you, and learn from you. God has so tightly knitted the threads of our ministries together that I'm not sure where one ends and the other begins. Something of you is lived out in me every single good day. You taught me countless things, like how to be not only a woman in ministry, but also a lady. Your love for Jesus the One and Only is wildly contagious. I am only one of many who caught it feverishly. How will I ever thank you for all you have invested in me? I love you dearly. Beth Moore, *Jesus the One and Only* (Nashville: LifeWay Press, 2000).

Heritage Keepers is another great ministry that is dedicated to encouraging and assisting women around the country. Its mission is to help women with their spiritual growth as well as equipping them to pass their faith on to the next generation. Lori Beckler and her husband, Bob, cofounded this ministry with great encouragement from Marge and many others. Marge continues to participate in Heritage Keepers events across the country. As a direct result, tens of thousands of women have grown in their faith and have committed their lives to passing it on to the next generation.

The list of those whose lives Marge has dramatically impacted would be a long one indeed. This woman of faith is a mentor and teacher from whom we all can learn.

Marge writes about the miracle of faith that enables us to become the persons God wants us to be.

The Miracle of Faith

The Bible tells us about the crippled man who sat by the gate called "Beautiful" in Jerusalem. He was badly crippled from birth. His family and friends took him every day and placed him at the gate, and he begged for everything he had.

Then one day—that started out just like any other—he saw two men walking toward him. Their names were Peter and John. I can see him now, peering up at them and wondering, *Man, are they going to give me any money?*

Wonder of all wonders. They stopped and stared at him. And then he heard Peter saying, "Silver and gold have I none; but such as I have give I thee: In the name of Jesus Christ of Nazareth rise up and walk" (Acts 3:6 KJV). And Peter stretched out his hand.

Did the man say, "No, sir, I can't do that. You see, I've never walked in my whole life and certainly can't start now. Why, my legs are all shriveled up and knotted, and I'm weak, and . . . and . . ."

Heavens, no! He reached out and took Peter's hand. Then his ankles received strength, and he began leaping for joy.

He didn't ruin a beautiful happening by making excuses. He took a firm grip and acted by faith. And a miracle happened.

It started out just like any other day. Jesus may send opportunity in the form of a friend, a telephone call, a note, a book, or perhaps even something we hear on the radio or see on TV. But the door cracks open. A miracle can happen to help you be the person you want to be. Marge Caldwell, *Speak Out with Marge* (Nashville: Broadman Press, 1976).

7

TARA DAWN
CHRISTENSEN

I was teaching the Sunday School
class gathered in the sanctuary
of a church in Brentwood, Tennessee, where Gene and I were guest
speakers that Sunday morning. I was
immediately drawn to a striking couple sitting in the back. He was tall,
handsome, and distinguished looking. She was a tall, beautiful brunette
who looked very familiar to me.
During the morning service I kept
glancing at her as she sang on the
back row of the choir. Where had

I seen her before? Finally, I leaned over to the person sitting next to me and asked her name. She said, "Don't you know? That's Tara Christensen—Miss America 1997. She and her husband, Jon (a former U.S. Congressman), attend church here regularly."

How refreshing to see this incredibly gorgeous and talented young lady who had earned a world-recognized title humbly blending into the worship service. Although she had sung an operatic aria for the talent portion of the Miss America pageant, on that Sunday morning Tara was simply singing in the choir for Jesus.

We talked with them after the service, and they invited us to their home that evening. It was a blessing to spend time with them as they shared their testimonies of God's hand in their lives. Although both of them are high profile personalities, it was soon obvious that their faith in God is their number-one priority. I was fascinated by Tara's story.

I started participating in pageants when I was a senior in high school. I wish I could tell you that my reason for entering pageants was completely God-centered, but that would be a lie. The fact is, I liked the idea of being on stage, performing in front of an audience, and, hopefully, winning a crown! However, God had a plan that went beyond my fascination with being a "queen."

I was 17 when I was given the opportunity to compete at the state level of the Miss America system. At the time, I lived in the state of Florida, and therefore, I participated in the Miss Florida Pageant. I was thrilled when I was named first runner-up.

Tara's eyes sparkled as she reflected on other competitions that led to her reign as Miss America. But it became clear that her dream to be Miss America evolved into a calling by God to make a difference in her world. She readily admits that gaining that title has resulted in doors of opportunity being opened to her. She gladly uses these opportunities to impact the lives of young people.

When she speaks privately and publicly, Tara takes a courageous stand for abstinence from premarital sex, and she also works diligently with crisis pregnancy centers. Some of the firm commitments and brave statements Tara and Jon have made are not always met with a friendly response.

Once, when Jon was running for governor of Nebraska, he was asked what was so special about Tara, his fiancée at that time. When he said that one of the extraordinary things was that she had saved herself for marriage, the media response was remarkable. Some of it was positive, but it evoked many derogatory comments, such as, "Who would want to marry someone who was sexually inexperienced?"

Dr. James Dobson invited Tara to be his guest on the *Focus on the Family* radio program. Her radiant, positive testimony was broadcast around the world, and her platform broadened enormously. She continues to speak out for abstinence to groups across the nation.

Tara and Jon work with First Priority, a campus-based ministry for middle and high school students. Their goal is to reach young people by uniting churches to equip students to reach their peers for Christ.

Even though her little-girl dream was to win crowns, glamour, and celebrity, God rearranged her goals. Somewhere in the midst of local and state competitions and the Miss America crown she won in Atlantic City, the desire for glitz and glory fell away as she surrendered to God's plan for her life. Her new message reflects His plan.

When I was younger, I thought I was the only person in the world abstaining from premarital sex. If I heard a message on abstinence, it was always from the point of view, "I made a mistake, and now I'm living with the consequences. Don't do what I did." I wondered if there was anyone else like me, because it seemed like no one was saving himself or herself for marriage. When I was crowned Miss America in 1997 and subsequently married Jon, many doors began to open for me to share my decision to remain pure. I love conveying to youth that they are worth waiting for. They can't change yesterday, but today can be a new start. Now, when I tell students that I was a 26-year-old virgin when I married Jon, I have the privilege of saying what I always wanted to hear someone say, "I waited, and so can you!"

God is using Tara as a mentor to this generation, changing her world as she teaches, *Whatever is true, whatever is noble, whatever is right, whatever is pure, whatever is lovely, whatever is admirable—if anything is excellent or praiseworthy—think about these things* (Phil. 4:8).

Today, Tara loves to remind women of all ages that inner beauty found through Jesus Christ is true beauty. It is not the Miss America crown but the crown of righteousness that catches the eye of a dark world.

8

MARTY COBB

The night seemed to go on forever, yet I dreaded what the morning would almost surely bring. I feared the worst as I watched my six-year-old son in his hospital bed. Again and again, the last few devastating hours filled my thoughts.

We were missionaries in South Korea—half a world away from our homeland. Stevie, the older of our two boys, always looking for adventure, had a tragic accident while playing on our mission station.

After climbing a high-tension electric tower, he was electrocuted and was now fighting for his life. He was terribly burned, and the damage to his kidneys and other internal organs was still undetermined. As I prayed over his little body, I wished I could turn back time and undo this awful day.

What if he didn't live? What if he did live? How could this have happened? We had allowed Stevie and his little brother to play in the woods behind our house; we thought it was a safe place. *Why didn't I think to warn him about possible dangers? What will we do without him?*

I sorted through precious memories of his short little life. I shed tears for my failures and feared for his little brother, Danny, who had seen the flames engulf his brother. I watched Stevie breathe, and I longed to scoop him up in my arms and hold him close. But I couldn't do that, because the doctors had told me that touching him would increase the risk of infection. With my eyes and words I tried to communicate my love for him.

Sometime the next day, a friend came to visit. She insisted that I take a break. I walked outside to a courtyard area. Alone, sitting on a concrete bench, I prayed for peace. My heart raced, and I felt that panic might swallow me. *It will be all right*, I heard. *I'm here.* The familiar presence surrounded me. My heart rate slowed as peace slipped in, and my faith in God was renewed. Whatever happened, I knew that our lives were under God's kind and loving control.

Within hours Stevie was moved by ambulance to a United States military hospital with the hope that he could be flown to a burn center in the States. A team of nurses and doctors were overseeing his care, and they encouraged my husband and me to go home and get some rest.

I took a shower and fell asleep. But at midnight my husband shook me awake. Someone from the hospital had called and asked us to come quickly. It was not good news. Stevie was not going to live much longer. He was just too badly injured, and there was no hope of recovery.

The streets of Seoul were nearly deserted as we made that dreaded trip. I leaned my head against the back of the seat and tried not to think about what awaited us. Before me appeared two strong arms. The Bible became real to me as the God of its pages stepped into my world. It was the most real thing I have ever experienced. As I placed my precious child into God's arms, I knew that he was safe forever.

The comfort and love of our friends and family surrounded me for the next few weeks. But eventually the reality of life without Stevie bore down upon me. *How could I live with this gaping hole in my heart?*

I randomly opened my Bible to Jer. 20:11 one day.

"I know the plans I have for you," says the Lord. "They are plans for good and not for evil, to give you a future and a hope" (TLB).

I felt a tingle in my fragile soul. *A future? A plan? Hope?*

For the rest of my life, these words will speak to my deepest need. I had felt very lost—without a plan and without hope for a future. But I realized at that moment that it's not about my plans. The plans are *His,* and they're good. He is hope. He controls the future. His plan for me is perfect and personal and filled with Him.

These words have held me up. They have been my shelter when the guilt and pain of our loss were more than I could bear. In His arms, even my tears became a healing balm that soothed my aching heart.

I remember sitting on my grandmother's porch swing when I was a girl. When the evenings turned cool, my grandmother brought her shawl and wrapped it around me. I was so happy and warm within the circle of her arms and her shawl. She's gone now, but that safe and secure feeling remains. Now God's personal presence surrounds me with strength and warmth that speak of His love, and I'm filled with a sense of acceptance and security.

God is with me—even in the extremes of life. He fills me with His amazing love and gives me hope and renews my faith. He has a good plan for my future, in which even the memory of my pain will be lost in His presence and in the shelter of His arms.

9

JANET
DAVIS

I was 12 years old, listening to a tender hymn of invitation "His Way with Thee." Tears of repentance and surrender erupted from my breaking heart and streamed down my innocent, adolescent cheeks. Love consumed me on that Sunday evening, and I committed my shredded life to Christ and His holy mission of feeding sheep. When I was six years old, the sudden death of my father had stunned my family into a life of shocking survival. The years of secret sexual molestation by a church deacon had left me feeling dirty, wondering why I had been this sick man's target. I felt so uncomfortable in my spirit, but a divine force with a still, small voice reassured, *I will never leave you or forsake you.* I clung to those words that I had needed to hear and chose finally to believe.

As sometimes happens, my attention slowly wandered away from the things of God toward the things the world offers. I became obsessed with the need to be loved by men and to quickly grow up and be a mom. Two marriages, two sons, and two divorces later, I was shattered by confusion, hopelessness, and despair. I sought relief in prescription drugs and alcohol. These provided short-term relief. The pain stopped only to return with an even stronger force of persecution and condemnation.

Chasing that temporary high became the focus of the next 20 years. Social drinking led to homelessness, then to drugs, and finally to prostitution as a means of financing my increasingly dangerous and expensive addiction. *Where was the God who promised He would never leave or forsake me? Who was this disgusting, filthy, diseased, skeleton who was once a vibrant ray of God's glory? How could I continue to live through such agony and abuse, praying for relief between tricks and fixes?*

I often thought of the God of my childhood as I stood at the bottom of the hill just down from the campus of Trevecca Nazarene University in Nashville. I remember wanting out of the hell I was living, but I was trapped in Satan's grip. Trevecca Community Church was located on the university campus, and the church's chimes resonated in my soul. I turned and saw the cross on the stained glass window, which reflected the rays of sun from heaven. I felt them penetrate my scarred face, I felt His warmth, and I heard His tender, pleading voice luring me home.

I was finally arrested one last time. Sick and secluded in a cell, I saw my reflection in a beaten tin mirror. *Who was that?* The image frightened me. I didn't even recognize myself. I had tried everything I knew to fill the vast hole in my soul, but what I really wanted was a fix of that love that I had experienced in my family's church on that special Sunday evening so long ago. Falling to my knees, I surrendered with the prayer I cried out that night and have repeated every day for more than three years now: *Lord, if you've allowed me to live, you must have purposed me to glorify you. Please change my heart.* And there it was, sweeping over and through this frail and broken vessel of His grace.

I left jail that time recognizing the angels that had always surrounded me, but now they had names. They provided me with love and mercy, manifested in a home, clean clothes, restored health, and renewed relationships. I returned to the sanctuary at Trevecca Community Church. The pastor, Dwight Gunter, told the story of Mary Magdalene, and I knew he was speaking to me. Once again I approached the altar, confessing to the Lord, *I'm a modern-day Mary Magdalene, and I need you so desperately.*

The divine hill of Trevecca became my new safe haven. I raised the rafters in praise on Sunday morning, and I enrolled in classes at the university. Thirteen months later, I walked across the commencement stage. It was still my body, but my soul belonged to Jesus.

Today, as I write this story, I've just seen the most beautiful portrait—a foggy ultrasound of a precious little embryo. Her name will be Anna Grace, and she'll arrive in the spring.

How amazing that my oldest son, Les—who once came to the street in an attempt to rescue me—will soon be a father and will welcome Gracie to the world and teach her to love and honor her granny! My prayer for forgiveness has been answered—forgiveness from my Lord and from my children.

God is everything to me. I thank Him for never leaving or forsaking me. All I want is for Him to have His way with me. I'm grateful for my mother's precious prayers and that she clung to that great promise "Train a child in the way he should go, and when he is old he will not turn from it" (Prov. 22:6).

10

MILLIE DIENERT

BY COLLETTE C. McBRATNEY

When I was in the eighth grade, my English teacher, Mrs. Frye, asked me to read a poem over the school intercom. Refusing her was not an option, so the coaching process began. She and I met after school so I could practice the poem. With her skilled guidance and encouragement, I did read it over the intercom—with only a few stumbles. Mrs. Frye saw me as a young lady with potential. She began with the end in mind. That's what mentors do. Thank you, Mrs. Frye, for helping me see possibilities.

Alice Blenner hired me as a training specialist. She said she knew I could do it, and she believed I would be an asset to her training and development team. Alice's faith in me launched my training career. She taught me how to write an effective project plan, design a dynamic workshop, and lead others. She's still a trusted friend. Thank you, Alice, for helping me reach for the stars.

A positive influence, such as a mentor, can be life-changing. The dictionary tells me that a mentor is a trusted counselor or guide; a tutor or coach. Mentors teach us today while touching our tomorrows.

In 1993 I lost my job and my dad, and the Lord knew I needed a spiritual mentor. I reconnected with Millie Dienert. I began attending her weekly Bible class in the Philadelphia area. Her Spirit-filled and candid teaching touched my heart. Millie pulls no punches; she is practical and humorous, and she models obedience. She has experienced many trials, tests, losses, and health limitations, but her faith remains firm.

I'm not sure mentors even realize what they're doing at the time. But when you meet one, you know it. Millie still mentors me. We talk about everything from fashion to faith. She has taught me life lessons and helped me be a better wife and a better friend.

Thank you, Millie, for investing in my life.

I've collected over the years what I call "Millie's maxims." Each is a short, salient thought that has enriched my life and nourished my soul. I've written many of them in my Bible. Here are a few:

Acceptance is *not* approval.

Attitude determines action.
Return telephone calls.
Give to God's work.
Let go of yesterday.
Read the Scriptures slowly.
Cultivate lasting friendships.
Pray for people you don't know.
Practice daily dependency on Him.
God never sees a crowd.

Are you mentoring someone? You may think you're not old enough, smart enough, or seasoned enough. But you are. Ask the Lord to lead you. In Christ you have what you need to be a godly mentor. He'll provide the courage, character, and conviction.

11

JUDY DOUGLASS

I've never been fond of heights. High places cause an actual physical shudder or flutter throughout my body. I was the one who kept the kids away from the edge of the scenic overlook. I couldn't stand to watch when my husband, Steve, took the children on the Ferris wheel. He loved to swing the chair just for me. I still use the inside lane when driving on high bridges, and I can't even comprehend why anyone would bungee jump. So it was breathtaking for me recently when the Lord told me to take a flying leap—of faith!

I have spent a lot of time with God lately seeking wisdom, strength, courage, faith—and clear direction—in light of my new responsibilities. My husband became the president of Campus Crusade for Christ International in 2001, replacing its founder and president of 50 years, Bill Bright. In Campus Crusade, husbands and wives work together, so Steve's new responsibilities had significant implications for me.

"Just relax," my husband encouraged me. "The job is impossible. Only God can do it."

I've consistently acknowledged that I'm unworthy and inadequate for this incredible privilege and opportunity. But God assures me that He has called me to it. So I've told Him that I'm His, and I'm totally available to be and do all He requires of me.

So I leapt—by faith. I don't know all I'll encounter. I don't know all that God is doing in my life, but He seems intent on doing some major refining. He has revealed only a glimpse of what He wants to do, but I know that my life is in His hands.

God has set me on a wonderful journey that has taken me to every continent. I've spoken with thousands of staff, initiating bold efforts to increase the training and opportunities for our staff women. It has included the most faith-stretching effort of my life: the Global Women's Leadership Forum.

Twenty-two women representing 11 nations met to design a gathering that would affirm our staff women in their value as women and significant contributors to our ministry. It was our desire to increase their confidence and ability to allow God to work through them to build movements of spiritual multiplication around the world.

Was the Global Women's Leadership Forum truly from God? Would others share our vision? Would the women come? Could we manage the logistical challenge of bringing together nearly 500 women from around the world? Could we design a program to meet our objectives? Where would we get the money?

God answered every question and every need beyond what we asked or imagined.

On March 9, 2004, in Chiang Mai, Thailand, the dream became reality. Nearly 500 women from 95 countries gathered to worship, to be encouraged, to develop their capacity to lead and to share and learn from one another.

In my 40 years of ministry, none of the efforts in which I've participated has been as thrilling as this one. God showed up in such a significant way. The women shared a sense of awe at the presence and blessing of God on our days in Chiang Mai.

The women worked with personal coaches and in teams to determine what their follow-through steps would be. Each one was challenged to return home and plant the seeds of leadership development, believing God for more than she could imagine in her sphere of influence.

Many staff women have sent me stories on their steps of faith, on the doors that are opening for ministry, and on the growth in their ministries and their leadership skills.

We have been thrilled with the potential of these women to serve God to their full capacity throughout the world.

I don't know where my next leap of faith will take me. But I do know this: My life is in God's hands.

12
KARLA
DOWNING

I vowed as a little girl to have a
good marriage, telling my mom
that I wasn't going to fight like
Daddy and her. When I met my
husband in church, I had been praying for a godly man, and I believed he
was God's choice. I wanted nothing
more than to serve God together and
raise our children in a Christian
home. It never occurred to me that
we would do anything but that.

My husband was also raised in
a dysfunctional home. Unaware that
we both brought childhood baggage
into our marriage, we were

unprepared to deal with the problems that immediately developed. I was devastated when we reacted to each other in destructive ways and created a home filled with turmoil and strife, not unlike my childhood home in many ways.

Desperately disappointed, I tried everything to force my husband to change. His response to my pushing, nagging, and arguing was to withdraw and control more. Expending all my energy to get him to see the problems resulted in my being out of control, all the while blaming him, believing that if he changed everything would be fine.

I searched the Bible to understand what God required of me, often confused about what God was doing in my life and why He allowed me to be in this situation. I struggled with submission, boundaries, fear, faith, and surrender. Many of the promises of the Bible seemed condemning, confusing, or elusive, only reinforcing my acute awareness that my marriage, home, and life didn't fit the "Christian" image. I often despaired at the lack of fruit in my life and felt like a failure as a Christian, too caught up in the daily dramas and emotional turmoil of my marriage to give God my all. I even felt guilty that I wasn't happy in spite of the circumstances. After all, wasn't God my true husband, and didn't He provide for all my needs?

For years, my desert journey seemed endless, dry, and barren. I often felt convinced that I married the wrong man and ruined God's plan for my life. I focused on my husband's failings and my disappointment.

Through the help of support groups, counselors, and books, I came to understand the dysfunctional dynamics that were affecting my marriage. We were both hurting from the past, so we were hurting each other and our children in the present. I learned that being a Christian did not remove the effects of the past or another person's sinful behavior, and I needed to deal with the problems in a different way.

I began to see my husband in a different light—not as a mean man intent on destroying me but as a broken and wounded man struggling the same way I was with a difficult childhood, hurt feelings, character strengths and weaknesses, and a sinful nature. This compassion allowed me to treat him with respect while taking care of myself and setting boundaries.

I understood that I was powerless over my husband and his choices, but not my own. I had been making the situation worse. Regardless of what my husband was doing, I needed to do what was right. I learned many difficult lessons: to accept things I couldn't change, to focus on myself rather than him, to refuse to respond to anger, to state my truth clearly and unapologetically, to set boundaries, to face fear, and to risk change. I needed to trust God in a new way, not just to change my circumstances and my husband but to take care of me no matter what happened to my marriage, even if that meant the worst outcome—divorce. A willingness to lose my marriage if things didn't improve resulted in a better marriage.

I had many regrets over what I felt were wasted years— the years when I should have productively served God and had a happy home instead of allowing myself to be consumed with my marriage problems to the exclusion of everything else. Then God began to stir up the gifts and talents He had given me and provided opportunities for me to reach out to comfort others with the comfort I had received. The spiritual, scriptural, and practical questions I struggled with over the years helped me to understand what other Christians need in their difficult relationships. The tools I learned, like "Detach with love," "Speak the truth in love," "Take care of myself," "Change myself, not him," "Reach out," "Set boundaries," and "Face my fears," were learned while wandering in the desert. I can now bring that survival pack to others still traveling there.

During the hardest days of my difficult marriage, I clung to Isa. 61:2-4, which says that Jesus was sent—

> to comfort all who mourn, and provide for those who grieve in Zion—to bestow on them a crown of beauty instead of ashes, the oil of gladness instead of mourning, and a garment of praise instead of a spirit of despair. They will be called oaks of righteousness, a planting of the LORD for the display of his splendor. They will rebuild the ancient ruins and restore the places long devastated; they will renew the ruined cities that have been devastated for generations.

The long-devastated places, the ruined cities, the ashes, the mourning, and the spirit of despair have all been replaced in my life with beauty, gladness, a display of God's splendor, and rebuilt relationships. The opportunities God has given me through my writing, speaking, and counseling to help others struggling in difficult relationships didn't come because I had the perfect marriage I wanted. The opportunities came because of the difficult marriage I didn't want. My ability to comfort others came directly out of the comfort I received while I was hurting and broken. The lessons I learned in my wilderness are now being shared with others, and I can look back and see God's hand in it all. Not only has He rebuilt my marriage (although it is still difficult at times)—He is also rebuilding others' lives and relationships through the ministry He has given me.

I have regrets, and in hindsight I would have done many things differently. But regardless of my mistakes, God works everything together for good for His purposes (see Rom. 8:28). My faith is strengthened by the ministry God formed from my brokenness and pain.

13
ALLYSON
FELIX

It was amazing to watch Allyson Felix representing the United States in the 2004 Olympics in Athens. She has become known as the world's fastest teenager. At just 18 years of age, Allyson broke world records in the 200-meter race and narrowly missed earning a gold medal. She captured the silver medal in the women's 200 meters on August 25 by setting a world junior record of 22.18 seconds. But more important than her speed and accomplishments is her strong Christian witness. In frequent interviews Allyson made it very clear that she sees her running ability as a gift from God.

Allyson's father, Paul, is an ordained minister and professor of New Testament at The Master's Seminary in Sun Valley, California. Her strong, supportive Christian heritage and family have been the basis of her testimony.

Because of her humble spirit and strong faith, when Allyson won the silver medal, she simply walked off the track. Her father said he was sure she would have taken a victory lap if she understood the significance of her accomplishment.

In repeated interviews, Allyson made it clear that her ability to run with such speed was a gift from God. And when she has encountered setbacks along the way, Allyson has stated, she's learned to depend on God. When she was recovering from injuries, she made it a practice each day to spend time in the Word and in prayer. Pastor Felix says that his daughter's faith is an important part of balancing the pressures that come with being a world-class runner. He told *Today's Christian,*

> We try to help Allyson keep things in perspective by looking at life from God's point of view. The reality is Allyson can get from point A to point B faster than most people, and our society has put a big emphasis on that. But that is not significant in light of eternity. So we try to remind her that God has given her this ability, and she is responsible for using it to His glory.

Allyson told the magazine, "My faith means everything to me, and in every way my goal is to bring God the glory."

Allyson's strong faith was passed on to her by her wonderful Christian family. She is living out her faith each day through her clear and vibrant testimony. But she's also committed to perpetuating the faith that has been handed to her through the courses she's taking at the University of Southern California. She's committed to sharing her faith with the next generation.

As I've read numerous interviews and articles about this remarkable young lady, I'm reminded of Paul's statement of purpose and determination:

> Since we are surrounded by such a great cloud of witnesses, let us throw off everything that hinders and the sin that so easily entangles, and let us run with perseverance the race marked out for us. Let us fix our eyes on Jesus, the author and perfecter of our faith, who for the joy set before him endured the cross, scorning its shame, and sat down at the right hand of the throne of God (*Heb. 12:1-2*).

Although Allyson's immediate goal is to be a world champion, as she runs life's race her eternal eyes are fixed on Jesus, the author and perfecter of her faith. Her stalwart testimony shows us that Allyson's ultimate goal is to crosses life's final finish line and say with Paul,

> I have fought the good fight, I have finished the race, I have kept the faith. Now there is in store for me the crown of righteousness, which the Lord, the righteous Judge, will award to me on that day (*2 Tim. 4:7-8*).

14

KAITLIN
FILLIPI

I have seen faith in many people —my mother, my grandmothers, even the people who used to watch me when I was a child. From years ago comes a photograph of me in a beautiful pink dress, holding a parasol. When I see that photograph, I'm always reminded of the love, prayers, and countless hours of sewing that Margie invested in me. I remember the "quiet purse" that Jan brought to church each Sunday to make church a fun place for a toddler. Amy, my best friend ever, always took the time to play and sing with me. The steadfast love and devotion of the people in our church makes me at home every time I step through the doors. My mother and grandmothers spent hours teaching, praying, playing, singing, and crying over me.

Each of these people has taught me the practical lessons of how faith in action operates. God doesn't want me to just sit back and keep my faith to myself. He wants to use me and is teaching me how to put my faith to work. Faith isn't meant to be kept just inside of us. It's meant to be shared with everyone we meet. I want to be a Jane, a Margie, and an Amy to others. I want to be the one who invests the countless hours crying, teaching, and playing into the lives of those around me.

Because of the faith that has been given to me, I can still quote with full confidence these words I wrote at the age of 14:

My Faith still stands through the trials of time,
My Faith still stands when life's heartbreak comes by,
My Faith still stands when I'm scared and alone,
My Faith still stands when I have nothing left to hold onto.
Because God is with me all the way, my faith still stands.

15

BLANCHE GRESSETT

When Pastor Joe Noonan called and asked me to paint the backdrop for our upcoming missions convention, it was easy to say yes. The hard part was agreeing to incorporate the theme of "touching our world" using the image of hands. I realized the urgency of sharing our faith with the world, and I told the pastor I would do my best even though I had never painted hands before. I promised to pray about it and see what the Lord showed me, because I knew I couldn't do it myself. Before hanging up, Pastor Joe said, "Let me pray with you right now." And he offered a simple prayer of faith, believing that God would inspire me.

During that prayer I felt touched by a beautiful presence. When he finished praying, I said, "I think I have an idea."

As soon as we hung up, I picked up my sketchpad. Quickly, a world, God's hand, and many hands reaching out began to emerge. For the next few days I constantly thought about hands—reaching and pointing. I purchased canvas and hung it on the wall of my studio. I prepared it with black acrylic paint.

A few days later, the Holy Spirit seemed to move me toward the canvas. I picked up my brush and began to touch the black with a blue oil color, leaving spaces at random for hands. Painting God's hand seemed the logical beginning point.

While I painted, I prayed. When I wiped my brush and stepped back to look, I was astonished. God's hand looked so real.

I drew a circle representing the world. White clouds emerged from my brush as it swirled across the surface, the world, and God's hand. I was in awe that He had inspired me to replicate His Creator hand—that hand that had first touched the world when He made it!

The hours flew by, and I took only short breaks. The paint continued to flow from my brush. As I worked clockwise, other hands began to appear. I was oblivious to everything else as the hands kept developing. Praying, believing, going from hand to hand, I rejoiced as each one appeared.

There were imploring hands, seeking and yearning; anxious, hurting hands; and a young child's hand that was balanced by an age-gnarled, twisted hand. Other hands were happy ones, bringing a message of faith and good tidings of great joy—touching the world with the Good News.

Transported, I kept painting, awed by the tangible presence of the Holy Spirit. The divine Artist continued to guide my hand as I painted, and the images seemed to appear involuntarily.

Finally, at about 2:00 A.M., I brushed the last stroke across the canvas and stepped back. It was at that moment that I became aware of the incredible symbolism. God had penetrated the blackness of a sin-darkened world when He stretched out His hand through the clouds with truth. He didn't create the world and then leave it; God remains involved, touching our world as He continues to bring light from darkness.

Exhilarated but totally exhausted, I fell into a deep sleep and slept for hours. When I finally awoke, my first thought was that the painting had just been a dream. I jumped up and ran to my studio.

As I stood before the canvas and studied it, tears filled my eyes. My heart was filled with a sense of deep humility and thanksgiving. God had indeed honored my faith by His presence and guidance and sent His angels to minister to me.

I called Pastor Joe and said, "You're not going to believe what God did for me!" He was as excited and happy as I was. When people came to my studio, they stood awestruck before the painting. It was obvious to everyone that this was a work of God.

Today, this painting has been across the United States and Canada and is now on display in Kansas City at the international headquarters of the Church of the Nazarene. It's a vibrant tribute to faith in God and our mandate to reach out to the lost and dying with the good news of Jesus Christ. When starving people reach out to Him, in faith believing, they're filled with the truth, never to hunger again!

16
BETHANY
HAMILTON

*B*ethany Hamilton has surfed the waves along the shores of Hawaii since she was tiny. So she was right at home on her surfboard on October 31, 2003. In a rare quiet moment as she lay on her board trailing her left arm in the water, she had no idea that her life was about to change.

Bethany saw a gray flash and the jaws of a 15-foot tiger shark. In an instant her left arm was gone, along with a chunk of her surfboard. A pool of blood appeared in the water surrounding her. With amazing calm, she told her friends nearby that she had been attacked by a shark. They took control of the situation, got her to shore, and then rushed her to the hospital. That sequence of events was the first in a series of miracles. Bethany's story has circled the globe and inspired millions with her unwavering faith.

Bethany's family loved the beach and surfing, and at the age of 13 Bethany was ranked as the number-one amateur female surfer in Hawaii.

In addition to her love of surfing, Bethany inherited a great tradition of faith. Her family is very close and loving, centered in God and church. She signs her personal note "In Christ" on her web site, at <www.bethanyhamilton.com>.

With her family's strong faith tradition, it's not surprising that from the moment the shark ripped off her arm, Bethany began praying over and over for God to help her. And He has been faithful.

Ironically, her dad was already prepped for knee surgery when she arrived at the hospital, and his room was used for her surgery. Two days later she endured a second surgery. The shock of seeing her stump for the first time almost caused her to faint, but she soon nicknamed it "Stumpy." Instead of wearing tops with sleeves, she prefers to wear tank tops. Her courage is an inspiration to everyone.

The day before Thanksgiving, Bethany gathered with her family and a few friends on a quiet beach and determinedly got back on her board. After a few attempts, she caught a wave and stood on her surfboard as she rode it back to shore. That was the beginning of her return to competitive surfing.

Bethany's faith in God has remained steadfast despite the challenges she has encountered. She has been bombarded with requests from media around the world. In an article in *USA Today*, March 19, 2004, the interviewer wrote, "Surprisingly, Hamilton doesn't view herself as strong, driven, or courageous. She sees the loss of her arm as her destiny, as a blessing in disguise."

Her father is quoted as saying, "Somehow God gave Bethany an amazing amount of grace in this. I am in awe. She never says, 'Why me?'"

A close family friend and family agent, Roy Hofstetter, says, "Bethany sees this as an opportunity handed to her by God. She believes that her arm was taken by the shark so she would be noticed and she could help and inspire others."

Her pastor, Steve Thompson, says, "Bethany's looking forward to the future. She's asking herself, 'How can I show the world I still have a life, that I enjoy my life and that my life is filled with joy?' She has an underlying trust that God is taking care of her."

Bethany says, "I might not be here if I hadn't asked for God's help. I look at everything that's happened as part of God's plan for my life, and I'm going to go with it."

When people ask her if she is afraid of sharks, she tells them that when she feels nervous she is reassured, because she knows that God is watching over her and that He'll take care of her.

Bethany feels a strong commitment to sharing her faith, especially with young people. She filmed a 30-second public service anti-drug message to be aired on radio and television stations across Hawaii. She has also been instrumental in raising funds to help disabled children around the world through World Vision. While Bethany was in New York for a series of interviews, she paused to give her jacket to a homeless girl on the streets and then cancelled a shopping trip, stating that she already had too many clothes.

After calling an eighth-grader in North Carolina who had lost an arm, Bethany was quoted in the December 2004 *Reader's Digest* as saying,

> Moments like this make me think I may be able to do more good having one arm than when I had two. I think this was God's plan for me all along. I'm not saying that God made the shark bite me. I think He knew it would happen, and He made a way for my life to be happy and meaningful in spite of it happening. If I can help other people find hope in God, then that is worth whatever I've lost.

Bethany's life and personal testimony remind the world that it doesn't take two arms to pass faith in God along.

17

JUDY
HEGSTROM

The first time I laid eyes on Paul Hegstrom was my first year of teen camp. During a class on dating and marriage, the leader asked us to think about the traits we would like in our spouses. When we were asked to share our thoughts, the only one to speak out was Paul. He made some crass comment, and the boys laughed. We girls thought he was a jerk. Two months later Paul moved to my hometown in Iowa and started attending my church.

Before long, Paul and I became an "item" in youth group. Our dating relationship was up and down, and I was constantly on edge. Nevertheless, when Paul insisted we get married while I was still a senior in high school, I agreed. My parents were against it, but they finally gave us their blessing, and we had a simple ceremony with just family members in attendance.

The day after our wedding was a Sunday—our first full day as man and wife. My brother was with us, and somehow he and Paul ended up in an argument. I tried to intervene, but Paul yelled, "This is none of your business!" He shoved me out of the room, and I fell. Suddenly I felt afraid of the person I had just married. Of course, he apologized. But he also added that it was really my own fault for interfering. And thus I began to accept blame for his abuse.

A few days later Paul criticized my intelligence.

"Too bad we all can't be as smart as you are," I retaliated. Paul backhanded me in the face, breaking my glasses. As the blood poured, my brother simply watched. Later Paul offered to take me to the hospital, but I was afraid of him and asked him just to take me to my parents' house.

Paul dropped me off in the driveway so that he wouldn't have to face my dad. I begged Dad not to hurt Paul—and thus I began to lay the foundation for excusing Paul's behavior.

Paul and I moved four times in the first few months of our marriage—twice to other towns. I worked at hamburger stands, and that was the main reason I ever had anything to eat. Finally, one day I called my dad to tell him I was hungry and wanted to come home. I didn't really want to go home— I just wanted Paul to get a job and take care of me.

Not long afterwards I found out that I was pregnant, and Paul and I moved to California. We moved continuously during our first years together. After our second daughter was born, I remember asking Paul if we would ever settle down and have a home of our own. He angrily informed me that we would have to sacrifice so he could return to college.

He did pursue a degree in theology in Oklahoma around that time, but I became pregnant again, and he dropped out of school. He tried to be a family man, but his old ways returned. He spent money frivolously and didn't pay our utility bills or buy food with what little money we did have. Our neighbors ran an extension cord from their garage into our home so that I could care for our children after dark. Paul was not the slightest bit embarrassed that others were providing for his family. He was just glad he didn't have to be responsible for us.

Paul was called to a church in a small community, and I hoped our lives would change. As our children grew up, I tried to protect them from his behavior, but, of course, they were aware of what was going on.

Instead of blaming Paul for his bad behavior, I blamed myself and tried to look perfect and perform perfectly. But nothing I did made him happy. The physical abuse continued to escalate. Once, while our children cried outside our locked bedroom door, Paul hit me so hard he knocked the wind out of me. The kids were screaming, asking if I was all right. I finally was able to tell them that I was fine, but they knew better. My children were not stupid—they were just helpless.

Eventually it became clear that Paul was seeing other women. He sometimes dressed up and left the house on holidays and Sundays to go to see "clients." I found pornography, and he said it belonged to a friend who had hidden it in our house.

My children and I barely survived. Sometimes Paul would be gone for long periods of time, and we were desperate for food. Social Services would not provide food stamps because Paul was earning money. A lady from our church was kind enough to bring us groceries. It was so humiliating that Paul was supposedly making good money but wouldn't take care of his family.

Paul continued to bounce in and out of our lives, but I was happiest when it was just the kids and me. Even when he lived away from us, though, he continued to control our lives. At one point our telephone was turned off because he hadn't paid the bill, but he still expected to talk to me every day and demanded that I go to a telephone two blocks away and wait for him to call.

We finally moved back together as a family. As I was unpacking boxes, I opened one that I thought contained household items. I found in it a folded paper, which I unfolded and read, "Hegstrom vs. Hegstrom." Unable to comprehend what I held in my hands, I called the attorney listed on the letterhead. He told me, "I'm sorry, Ma'am, but you're divorced."

The attorney explained that Paul had said he didn't know where I lived or how to contact me so he had been awarded an uncontested divorce from me.

The children and I found a new apartment of our own and began to enjoy newfound freedom. I grappled spiritually with why God hadn't changed Paul and why I had suffered so much in my relationship with Paul. Then one night the Lord spoke to me. *Don't pray for Paul to return. Pray for his soul.*

After weeks of praying for Paul and giving him to God, I realized that I no longer had feelings for him. I was able to continue with my life alone. I began to see myself as a valuable person, capable of using my brain and acceptable to myself and others. The years passed smoothly.

When our younger daughter was ready to leave for college, I was afraid my car wouldn't make the 500-mile trip. I swallowed my pride and asked Paul if he would let me borrow his car to take her. He told me he and his girlfriend had broken up for good, although I didn't believe him and didn't really care. He said he didn't want me to drive that far alone and that he would take Heidi to school. I knew she wouldn't feel comfortable alone with him, so I said I would go along too.

On the drive home from taking her to college, Paul and I talked like normal human beings. There were no put-downs, no blaming. I wondered what in the world had happened to him. He told me he had been in therapy and that his attitudes were changing. He was beginning to accept responsibility for his past behavior.

He started inviting me to meet him for coffee occasionally. We weren't dating—just talking. I left our talks feeling like a normal person. I could discuss things with him without his becoming angry. It didn't seem to affect him adversely when I didn't share his opinions on everything.

Eventually we were seeing each other regularly, but I was still cautious. One day he asked me if I had ever thought about getting back together. I told him I thought about how different things might have been if he had been like this when we were married. I told him I could tell he had been working on himself and that I really liked the new guy. He seemed to be proud when I said that—but humble at the same time.

I asked God for direction. Soon I began having feelings of love for Paul that I had never felt during our marriage. Paul told me he was having the same feelings and that even though he was afraid, God had shown him that our family would be restored.

The weeks following our second wedding were wonderful. He was truly a changed man. The years of our second marriage have been very happy ones. Although I've had to face some unresolved feelings and insecurities left over from our first marriage, I now live a happy, abuse-free existence with my husband.

Paul and I have learned so much, and it's our desire to share what the Lord has taught us on our journey. God provides help for us through the Bible and His people. If you are an angry man, or a woman who loves an angry man, it is my prayer that you will benefit from our story.

18

LIZ CURTIS HIGGS

esus said to [Martha], "I am the resurrection and the life. He who believes in me will live, even though he dies; and whoever lives and believes in me will never die. Do you believe this?" (John 11:25-26).

When I had been married to Bill for all of eight months and was still not pregnant, I sought out a new doctor to see if everything was OK. *What if I can't bear children after all?* I fretted. *What if something isn't right?*

After a thorough examination, the doctor and I met in his office to discuss the results. Gently, he laughed away my concerns. "You're perfectly healthy, Liz. Why are you so worried about conceiving? It's only been eight months."

I hesitated and then began sharing a few details of my promiscuous past with him. "Doctor," I confessed, "I have this terrible fear that, with all those partners over all those years, I may have done some irreparable damage."

"Ohhh," he said, his eyes wide. "I, uh—appreciate your honesty." I could see he was trying hard not to be shocked. I assured him, my voice becoming more confident, "I'm a Christian now, and I've been forgiven for those old sins."

"Aha!" he said suddenly, with a triumphant gleam in his eye. "If you're a Christian, then you can tell me how you know beyond a shadow of a doubt that the Resurrection really happened, that Jesus rose from the dead."

Boy, did that come out of left field! Gulp! This must be what Paul meant when he told Timothy to be ready to speak the truth in season and out of season. One of those seasons had just sneaked up on me!

"Well?" the doctor asked, leaning across his desk with expectation in his eyes.

I took a deep breath, and with it came an immediate sense of peaceful assurance as the words I needed flowed from my heart and lips: "I know that Jesus is raised from the dead because He raised *me* from the dead."

There it was, simple, powerful, and undeniable. Pretty obvious where that much-needed explanation came from too. I smiled and sent a silent prayer heavenward: *Thanks, Lord!*

But the doc wasn't finished yet. "Tell me more!" he insisted. And so while up and down the hall a dozen women in flimsy paper dresses waited for their physician to show up, I shared with him the basic truths of the Resurrection—namely, that Jesus is in the business of raising people from the dead. Was then—is now. Stay tuned—more to come.

Lord, help me always be prepared to give a reason for my hope. Fill me so completely with the reality of you that anytime, anywhere, I can respond as Martha did:

"Yes, Lord. I believe."

19

HOPE
HINSON

When I was in the seventh grade, I made the promise to God to save my virginity for my husband. However, at the time I didn't understand the depth of the covenant I made. I was with my youth group and my best friend and simply felt that making this promise was what I was supposed to do. My parents had instilled in me wonderful Christian morals and standards, especially in presenting myself as a lady in public and in secret. However, my interpretation of what it meant to be pure was to abstain from sex until marriage. Many emotional and physical scars later, I realized that my definition of purity was a damaging misunderstanding.

I am 21 years old, and I'm a virgin. This is my claim to purity, right? In the years that I've held on to that claim—and I continue to hold it—that's what I believed. I had many boyfriends, and I felt that love was getting to know everything there was to know about each other: mentally, emotionally, and most important, physically. I felt that the more they knew me physically, the closer I was to true love and happiness. As relationships ended, I was left with an ache of emptiness, guilt, and worthlessness. What was wrong? I didn't have sex with them. Why did it hurt so badly? True, I was holding on to my virginity, but I felt constant remorse for the little things I had done. There were times when I stepped right up to the line and mocked purity by indulging in heavy petting and make-out sessions. I allowed casual boyfriends to know the most intimate parts of me. I rationalized these infractions by telling myself that I wasn't going all the way. But I didn't feel pure. I was left with scars that would taint my perception of my future mate and even my feeling of self-worth. As the months and years went by, the Lord began to reveal to me the real meaning of purity. With that new knowledge came a desire to share with other young women what I had learned.

I learned that purity goes further than just saving oneself for marriage. By God's grace, I have embraced this reality. There are many books available on purity that have been written by women who are now married. Their stories are powerful, but it's hard for me to relate to them. I'm guilty, forgiven—and still single.

There are no formulas for the perfect life. But I can say with great excitement that I'm being richly blessed in my singleness, and I'm keeping my treasure wrapped tightly and securely for my future mate.

Our Father has planned for us lives full of much more than shady boundaries and guilty consciences. But sometimes we search for our identity in the wrong places. We're more than the sum of our material possessions and physical relationships. And He doesn't want us to live in the shadow of yesterday's mistakes. At the throne of grace we can find our reflection in the eyes of the Savior—the one who sees our sin and still loves us.

Healing and restoration are available for the girl lost in a life of impurity. There's more for young women than what's offered on the pages of *Seventeen*. Life, love, and completeness are found in the Savior who saves, redeems, and is waiting to hold His daughters close to Him.

20

SHIRLEY HORNER

A few years ago I picked up a book titled *The Things I Wish I Had Known*. I remember thinking that if I ever wrote a book, I would title it *All the Things I'm Glad I Didn't Know*.

I'm thankful I didn't know childbirth was really painful. I'm a wimp when it comes to needles and pain. I might not have experienced the blessings of my two children and three grand-children if I had known the pain of giving birth.

I'm thankful I didn't know a good marriage is a work in progress. I might have remained single, and I would not have learned the meaning of "the two shall become one."

I'm thankful I didn't know that one of my children would walk away from God for a season. I would not have learned to rest in Isa. 49.

I'm thankful I didn't know that my career would be such a challenge that I would be tempted to give up. I would not have been in a position to draw upon the strength known by the Bible heroes of my childhood.

I'm thankful I didn't know that in 2002 I would awaken from "routine" surgery and learn that not all the cancer had been removed. I would have missed the peace of restored faith.

With cancer came the hated questions: *Is this it? Am I going to die?* As I prayed, my fears faded, and I was able to refocus. I began to search the Internet to research metastasized ovarian cancer, and I developed a plan to avoid chemotherapy. A few weeks later I was asked to speak at a national conference. I was excited for the opportunity to publicly share what Jesus was doing in my life.

When I met with an oncologist, he said, "At this time I'm not going to recommend chemotherapy or radiation." I felt that God had gone before me. My last doctor's report was a good one, and I'm not scheduled for more tests until six months from now.

Yes, I'm thankful we don't know in advance all the bumps that lie in the road ahead. What I'm glad to know is that God's grace is sufficient.

21

BARBARA JOHNSON

Barbara Johnson epitomizes faith. Known through her writing and public speaking as "the geranium lady" and "the queen of encouragement," Barbara has reached millions with hope in the midst of despair.

Barbara has battled poor health, personal loss, financial setbacks, and many other challenges. Yet she has graciously guided me through the pitfalls of publication.

During a recent phone conversation, we reviewed the litany of her crises—the death of her husband, a malignant brain tumor, diabetes, two broken arms, numerous hospitalizations, and so on. Just two weeks prior, she had endured eye surgery necessitated by lymphoma cells, and her eyesight is threatened. To top it off, she was in bed with a case of shingles.

"I'm in so much pain I have to stay in bed and try not to move," she told me. "I can't drive and can barely walk or see." She paused a moment. "But there *is* good news! I'm not pregnant!"

My amazing friend can still find the silver lining. She's a picture of James 1:2—"Consider it pure joy . . . whenever you face trials of many kinds."

Barbara tells us in her book *Laughter from Heaven*, "If you pursue happiness, it will elude you. But if you focus on your faith, your family, your friends, the needs of others, your work, and do the very best you can, happiness will find you."

Thank you, Barbara, for your legacy of joy and faith.

22

ANNE GRAHAM LOTZ

When the telephone rang on February 26, 1998, I had no idea the call would precipitate a launch into the wild blue yonder of faith. My son's voice on the other end of the line sounded strong but serious. "Mom, the doctor thinks I have cancer."

With those few words, I was suddenly catapulted into the eye of an unexpected, raging storm of suffering that lashed at every aspect of my life.

One of my priorities as a mother had been to make sure my children were safe. When they were small, I carefully strapped them into their car seats, held their hands protectively when walking, made sure the medicines and cleaning products were safely out of reach, and barricaded the steps or other areas where they might hurt themselves. As they grew up, I made sure I knew who their friends were, where they spent their time, and what they were being taught in school. I carefully helped them select television programs, movies, and reading material that would be fun and stimulating but would not damage their minds or spirits. I gave them prayerful, thoughtful counsel on their choices of where to go to college, whom to marry, what jobs to take, and where to live. But what could I do in the face of cancer? Never had I felt so helpless!

Yet in the midst of the storm that hit as suddenly and fiercely as a devastating tornado, I experienced an unprecedented peace—and joy! Because I knew that while I was helpless in myself, I could lay hold of the one who is mighty and whose faithfulness surrounds Him. (See Ps. 89:8.) So with tears streaming down my cheeks, I prayed with my son, Jonathan, on the telephone during that initial conversation. I was able to praise God for His divine purpose for my son's life. Although we had been caught by surprise, I knew God had known about it since before Jonathan was born. I knew also that he had been prayed for before conception, every day of my pregnancy, and every day of his life since birth. He had been born again into God's family when he was a child, and now as a young adult he was in God's will as far as he understood it. Therefore I had absolute confidence that this suffering would be for Jonathan's good and God's glory. (See Rom. 8:28.)

So on the telephone Jonathan and I prayed together, recommitting his life for the purpose of glorifying God. We acknowledged that he would bring God glory through faithfully trusting Him if the cancer led to death, the cancer went into remission, the cancer was surgically and successfully removed, or if the cancer simply disappeared. When I hung up the telephone with tears on my face, a lump in my throat, and an ache in my heart, I knew I was soaring higher in faith than I ever had before.

In the next few hours, which seemed like years, the doctor's diagnosis was confirmed by the examination of a specialist. Within a week of the first diagnosis, and just four weeks before his wedding day, our 28-year-old son underwent successful surgery to remove a malignant tumor. After completing the recommended follow-up treatments of radiation, Jonathan's prognosis for total recovery has been excellent.

As grateful and thrilled as we still are over this answer to our prayers, we know the real victory was won not on the surgeon's table but on the telephone, in prayer, as we agreed to trust God with whatever the outcome might be.

23
HENRIETTA
MEARS

Billy Graham said Henrietta Mears was one of the greatest Christians he had ever known. And Henrietta was a major mentor to Vonette and Bill Bright.

Who was this woman? Bill Bright said in his book *What Jesus Is All About* that she "directly discipled hundreds of young people whom God led into full-time Christian ministry. Today, no doubt the thousands of disciples they influenced are, in turn, introducing millions of people to Christ. Henrietta's life was one of spiritual multiplication, and the world is a better place in which to live because she surrendered her life as a young woman to the Lord Jesus Christ to serve Him with all her heart."

Everyone who met Henrietta Mears knew that her faith in God was paramount in her life. She wasn't afraid to trust God regardless of how difficult the circumstances might be. Because of her unswerving faith in God, she dreamed big, and God used her to impact the lives of thousands of young people around the world.

Henrietta learned the essence of mentoring at the feet of her mother, to whom she attributed her strong faith and early devotion to Christ. She learned to dream big as she trusted the Lord with her whole heart. As a result, her entire life was devoted to knowing Christ intimately and telling others about Him.

She never married, and she treated her singleness with humor. When asked about her marital status, she often responded that the apostle Paul was the only man she could have married, and he didn't wait for her.

Henrietta loved young people and was most at home with them and her Bible. She was overjoyed when she was asked to become the director of Christian education at First Presbyterian Church in Hollywood, California, in 1928. In three years under her guidance, Sunday School attendance at that church grew from 450 to more than 6,000, and more than 400 young people at the church entered full-time Christian service.

When Henrietta discovered that the Sunday School material wasn't in keeping with her convictions and studies, she started writing the lessons herself—lessons that were bold, challenging, and captivating and presented the basic tenets of God's Word.

As word of the phenomenal growth and obvious results of her efforts spread, requests for copies of her study material came in from around the country and ultimately around the world. It wasn't long before the demand became too great, and Henrietta and a number of businessmen established Gospel Light Publications, a pioneer in the field of Christian publishing.

Henrietta was able to purchase a privately owned resort in the San Bernardino Mountains that became the Forest Home Conference Center, where retreats were held that were filled with activity and laughter and evenings packed with spiritual insight. Thousands of lifetime commitments to Christ were made in the outdoor amphitheater by a blazing bonfire. Patiently and prayerfully, Henrietta discipled.

Many came to know Christ as a result of Hollywood Christian Group, a ministry begun by Henrietta that met in her home. Colleen Townsend, a young actress under contract with Twentieth Century Fox, began attending, and through the witness of the group's members—especially that of a young man named Louie Evans—she sensed her own spiritual need. Colleen and Louie were married and have had an incredible ministry over the years. Once mentored by Henrietta, Colleen has mentored thousands through her speaking and writing.

Vonette Bright was led to faith in Jesus Christ by Henrietta Mears. Vonette and her husband, Bill, founded Campus Crusade for Christ. They lived with Miss Mears for a time. Vonette says, "I caught from Henrietta Mears, as from no other woman, the Christian life—not only from her teaching but also from her living. Daily I drew from her personality the vibrant, positive, practical, persuasive words and lifestyle that God allowed to penetrate my life. To me she was one of the greatest Christians of all time. She generously shared her life with Bill and me, and that caused us to love and appreciate her for what she truly was—a woman of God."

Bill and Vonette impacted additional millions for Christ—including me.

In 1949, Dr. Mears's path crossed that of young evangelist Billy Graham. At the time, he was experiencing a crisis in his soul and shared with Henrietta some of his concerns about the Los Angeles Crusade that was ahead of him. He later said, "Henrietta Mears had a remarkable influence on my life. In fact, I doubt if any other woman outside of my wife and mother has had such a marked influence. Her gracious spirit, her devotional life, her steadfastness for the simple gospel, and her knowledge of the Bible has been a continual inspiration and amazement to me. She is certainly one of the greatest Christians I have ever known."

The list of those influenced by Henrietta Mears includes actors, politicians, leaders, and pastors. Upon her death in 1963, someone remarked, "It's nothing new for her to meet her Lord alone, because she often did so. Today He decided to keep her with Him."

From her mother's knee to her last breath, Henrietta Mears chose to spread her faith to everyone around her. May we, like her, be mentors of our faith.

24

MOTHER TERESA

Mother Teresa is one of the great heroes of faith. Her life deepened my faith in God and inspired me to believe the impossible can be accomplished.

She didn't look like a hero. In her unpretentious white sari, Mother Teresa remained a persistent symbol of selflessness. With her gnarled hands and wrinkled and careworn face, her stooped and wizened figure stood alone against the frenzied quest for eternally smooth-skin agelessness.

Her lovely magnificence shone from deep within as she invested her life in the enhancement of her inner beauty. Her desire was to reflect the love and radiance of her Father. Though she lived modestly and walked a simple path, her faith made a great impression on the world.

Mother Teresa radiated the love of God wherever she went. Whether she was on the streets of Calcutta holding a dying leper or receiving a Nobel Prize, she unswervingly shared her faith in God and her love for the poorest of the poor and the lowliest of the low. A beggar clad in rags and cast into the gutters of the streets of our world became her cherished child. Time after time, she gathered the dying in her arms and took them with her to a place where they could breathe their last breath with dignity. She saw herself as a missionary commissioned to deliver God's love and compassion to the hungry, the naked, the homeless, and the dying.

One of the basic tenets of Mother Teresa's life was prayer. She believed that faith is the fruit of prayer. As a vessel of good and of God, she saw Jesus in every person. She never spared or coddled herself. Wearing out several pacemakers, she seemed indestructible. She gave herself sacrificially, always thinking of others first.

Mother Teresa told people that when she touched a leper's arm she was touching Jesus. Her single-minded devotion to the cause of caring for outcasts crossed all parochial and denominational lines and religious styles. She exemplified the life of holiness and self-sacrifice. "Holiness is the simple duty of all," she said. "Holiness is for everyone." By that she meant that it is not just those called to full-time Christian service who are expected to live godly lives—*every* Christian must be centered in Christ to be whole. She knew that complete surrender to God is the most essential ingredient of the Christian life.

Mother Teresa's solid faith in God was learned as a peasant child growing up in what is now Yugoslavia. When she left home, her mother told her, "You go, put your hand in Jesus' hand, and walk alone with Him." Her mother's love for Jesus was paramount.

Mother Teresa's path took her down narrow alleys and into throne rooms of reigning monarchs. Everywhere she went she told people to touch a leper with kindness.

Mother Teresa took a vow of poverty in order to understand the conditions of those whom she served. She said, "The more we have the less we can give. Poverty is a wonderful gift because it gives us freedom—it means we have fewer obstacles to God." For her, no sacrifice was too great. Although her solitary path may have appeared lonely at times, her faith in God sustained her, and it was obvious that He was close beside her at all times.

Speaking from a heart that had been filled with the wisdom of God, Mother Teresa distributed pearls of hope and challenged all of us. She founded the Missionaries of Charity to minister to the destitute.

A reporter once asked her what she did for the dying and hopeless. She told him that the first thing she did was make them feel wanted. Even if it was the last hours of their lives, she showed them her faith in God and demonstrated His love as she cared for them.

Mother Teresa believed that each of us can model our faith in God by becoming pencils in His hands. In her quiet, simple way, she shined the light of the Son of God into the darkest corners of the world. It didn't matter to her whether she was touching the smooth, healthy skin of a king or the bony, leathery skin of a dying leper. She reached out to presidents and European royalty as well as beggars. Wherever Mother Teresa went peace was found and hope restored.

Once she was asked what she hoped to hear when the time came for her to die. She quoted from Matt. 25:

> Come, you who are blessed by my Father; take your inheritance, the kingdom prepared for you since the creation of the world. For I was hungry and you gave me something to eat, I was thirsty and you gave me something to drink, I was a stranger and you invited me in. . . . Whatever you did for one of the least of these brothers of mine, you did for me (*vv. 34-35, 40*).

When Mother Teresa died she left only a worn prayer book, a rosary, two blue and white saris, a bucket, and a rough sponge. Her treasures were intangibles of unconditional love, compassionate kindness, and undaunted courage. Throughout her life she distributed those priceless riches as she caressed and cared for the forgotten ones. Her investments are eternal and were stored in heaven.

"I believe in interacting person-to-person," Mother Teresa said. "Every person is Jesus Christ for me. And since there is only one Jesus, that person is the only person in the world for me at that time." When asked for the reason for her success, she always replied, "I have done nothing. Jesus has done it all!"

25
JANET
MUSEVENI

I was privileged to meet and inter-
view First Lady Janet Museveni
of the Republic of Uganda in 2002.
She is a profoundly influential
Christian woman.

Her husband, Yoweri Museveni,
became president of Uganda in 1986
and has personally spearheaded
campaigns to inform and educate the
population about the AIDS epidem-
ic. The first lady has been his co-
leader and his staunchest supporter
in this campaign.

Yoweri and Janet Museveni's message emphasizing sexual abstinence outside of marriage, plus faithfulness between marriage partners, has resulted in a 15-percent decrease in the spread of the HIV virus throughout the republic. They also work to overcome the myth that condoms are a completely reliable means of stemming the tide of AIDS and believe that line of thinking promotes immorality and a false sense of protection. Mrs. Museveni founded the Uganda Youth Forum, an organization committed to training the younger generation by instilling values and discipline that provide the framework of a moral lifestyle.

Many strategies to fight AIDS have been implemented, but it's clear that the most important strategy is education and prevention. More than 80 percent of Ugandans now know what AIDS is, how it's transmitted, and how to avoid it. However, head knowledge is not enough, so the Museveni administration is committed to working relentlessly so its citizens will understand the importance of changing their lifestyles.

Mrs. Museveni spoke in February 2002 at the Prescription for Hope Conference in Washington, D.C., sponsored by Samaritan's Purse. She said,

> In Uganda we have learned that unless we reverse the trends, with God's support, nobody else can do it for us. I stand here today in all humility to tell you that we indeed have worked hard, believing as you all do that we have the duty and means to change things, and many things have changed. The fight against HIV/AIDS is one such change.

The first lady acknowledges that it's hard to change the behavior of adults. However, she knows that it's relatively easy to shape the behavior of the young, and they're doing this through the school system and mass media. She's also aware that in order for their efforts to be successful, they must be undergirded by the principles of the Word of God.

Because of the AIDS crisis in Uganda, the number of children left without parents is staggering. Mrs. Museveni founded the Uganda Women's Effort to Save Orphans, an organization that has had a positive effect on 65,000 orphans in the past 15 years.

The story of redemption in the Republic of Uganda continues. First Lady Janet Museveni is a modern-day Esther, committed to saving her people. She courageously has devoted the influence God has given her to bettering the quality of life in Uganda.

26

LAUREN
OCHS

As I was growing up, church was a Sunday ritual for my family, and I was blessed with a rich spiritual heritage that established a lasting foundation for my faith. The depth of spiritual influence ran deep. My parents and grandparents taught the importance of truth, love, giving, and eternal outlook on life, and they also lived out those values on a daily basis.

My parents believe in the value of Christian education, and they sacrificed to make that possible for me.

The acts of love, the time they spent on their knees, and their example of trusting God in hard times showed me faith and love in action. It's much easier to follow what someone does rather than to simply do what he or she says.

The first 22 years of my life have been built on the legacy my family created. I realize that it's time to determine my own legacy. I dream of finding the perfect husband and starting my own family. I pray that I'll have the chance to pass my faith to future generations.

I also want to leave a legacy that touches every person with whom I come in contact. I may not be remembered for my accomplishments, but I hope to be remembered as a woman who loved the Lord, believed God's Word, and let my beliefs affect every aspect of my life.

I want to live Deut. 6:5-7: "Love the LORD your God with all you heart and with all your soul and with all your strength. These commandments that I give you today are to be upon your hearts. Impress them on your children. Talk about them when you sit at home and when you walk along the road, when you lie down and when you get up."

27

MELODY
PADGETT

My family worshiped the devil. As a young girl, I was repeatedly abused sexually by a relative. My parents didn't do anything about it, because they didn't want to start trouble with the whole family. I learned early on that whatever happened to me, I had to deal with it on my own.

I was the oldest of four children. My dad worked the 3-11 shift, and my mother went out most nights with another man, leaving me in charge at home. I was nine years old, but she thought that was old enough to take care of the other kids, the cooking, and the cleaning. She left the house most days at 4:00 and I had to make sure my brothers and sister were in bed before she got home at 10:30.

When I was 18, my parents forced me to marry a fellow they liked even though I didn't want to marry him. He abused me, but my parents said it was my fault. They took his side every time. We had three children, who mean the world to me.

My husband came home from work one day and told me and the children that we would have to leave. My parents disowned me, and we had no place to go. We ended up staying in an old, run-down recreational vehicle for about a year.

I found a job and worked when my children were in school, and we were finally able to move into a house. About this time my husband decided he wanted the children, and he took me to court to gain custody. I won the case, but when my husband spent time with the kids, he turned them against me. By the time they were teenagers they were out of control. The children told me often that they hated me and wished I were dead. My own children forced me out of the house, and I had to live in my car. I wanted to die.

I attempted suicide and ended up in a coma for three days. I remember being angry when I woke up because I didn't want to live. I hated everyone.

My children were sexually active and using drugs. My youngest son was even getting into trouble with the law. In May 2001 I received a call at work one day informing me that he was going to be sent to San Antonio for help. I stood there holding the phone and crying. A lady named Leah asked me what was wrong, but I didn't want to tell her—I still believed that I was supposed to fix my own problems.

One day Leah approached me again and asked if there was any way she could help me. I ended up telling her everything, and she listened patiently. She asked me about my relationship with the Lord. I wondered why she was trying to tell me about somebody I didn't even know or care about. But because she was so nice to me, I listened.

Leah invited me to go to church with her. It took a couple of weeks to get up the courage to go, but I finally went with her to church on May 27, 2001, two days before my 39th birthday. At the end of the service, I went to the altar with Leah and gave my heart to the Lord. I knew at that moment that God was living in me. In my excitement, I told my parents what had happened to me. They were angry because I gave my heart to Jesus rather than Satan. But nothing they said could take away the joy and peace I found that day.

It's been a battle serving the Lord, but it's been worth it. One evening as I was walking to church, I was attacked by a pit bull. I was knocked to the ground, and my dress was torn. But I got up and went right on to church. When my daughter heard about the dog attack, she told the neighbors, "Mom don't miss church for nothin'!"

I often wrote to my son who was in San Antonio, and I sent Bible verses every time I wrote. After a little more than a year, he gave his heart to the Lord. One of the verses I sent him was Rom. 8:28—"In all things God works for the good of those who love him, who have been called according to his purpose."

I've been a Christian for two years now, and I love learning about the Lord. Leah has become one of my closest friends, and the people at church have accepted me and make me feel welcome.

As I look back over my life, I know that God was protecting me before I even knew Him. Because I have the Lord in my life, I know that I will make it. "I can do everything through him who gives me strength" (Phil. 4:13).

28

CHONDA

PIERCE

*R*ock Hill, South Carolina, is a small town snugly situated near the North Carolina state line, near Charlotte. It was the site of my dad's first pastorate. We moved from Kentucky in 1964 and discovered a new church family. The church and the parsonage were side by side. I think the same contractor must have built both buildings; they looked almost identical. There was only one way to tell them apart: the church had a steeple, and the parsonage didn't!

Well, actually one night while Mom and Dad were doing church visitation, we tried to burn down the parsonage. Mike and Charlotta carried Cheralyn and me into the hall closet to tell us ghost stories. The story was scary, but not as frightening as the sight of orange-and-yellow flames dancing up the sleeve of one of my mother's hanging coats. I suppose we shouldn't have lit those candles for special effect.

Charlotta carried Cheralyn, while Mike dragged me across the snow-covered front lawn to the house across the street to call the fire department. Luckily, the house suffered only minor smoke damage. My brother was the most exciting baby-sitter I ever had! Despite my vote of confidence, Mike was fired (no pun intended). It was a while before we were left alone again.

The church folk from Rock Hill provided my first experience with a church family—a family I'll never forget. I can still see Brother Pea, who always passed out dimes to the preacher's kids every Sunday morning. He had once had skin cancer on his face, and consequently a portion of his cheek had been removed. The surgery had left a small opening about the size of a pea in his cheek. (I always wondered if that's where he got his name, but Mother wouldn't let me ask.) I also remember Grandma Simmons, who lived in a white house behind the church. She was the first "aisle runner" and "glory shouter" I ever knew. It just hadn't been a good revival if Grandma Simmons hadn't shouted and run the aisles.

My most special memories in Rock Hill are of Aunt Doris. Every preacher's kid needs an Aunt Doris—especially a preacher's middle kid.

At that time in my life I shared a bedroom with my two sisters. Charlotta had grace and talent on her side. Everyone seemed to dote over her long, blonde hair (always curled in ringlets), her extraordinary musical abilities, and her sweet

poise and manners. Cheralyn was the "baby." Need I say
more? Who can compete with a baby? She toddled around
our little home as if she owned the place! She was remarkable—beautiful dark eyes, olive skin, yet with soft, bright
blond hair. Her only physical flaw was her nose, which was
always skinned up. But even that turned into her advantage.
It just meant more lollipops at church and more to-do over
her little "boo-boo." And even though I idolized my brother
Mike, he was "too cool" to be seen with a kid sister.

But I had Aunt Doris—and Aunt Doris had me! She let
me sleep over at her house all by myself. She fixed my fa-
vorite foods and always seemed to have a little surprise in her
purse at church—just for me. She would pick me up Saturday
afternoons and take me to Rose's Department Store. There I
could get a piece of candy (that I didn't have to share), a stick
of bubble gum, and ride the electric pony—all for a nickel!

Aunt Doris was not related to my family, but going to
her house anytime was as wonderful to me as going to
Grandma's house at Christmastime. She was so special. And
she was my Sunday school teacher too. Aunt Doris made me
feel like the most important little girl in the world.

I ran into Aunt Doris a few years ago, and my heart
jumped. All it took was her sweet arms around my adult
shoulders for me to feel like that special little girl again! We
reminisced about our Rock Hill church family. I was so happy to be able to introduce her to my daughter. I wanted
somehow for that same magic that was poured out onto me
to flow onto *my* little girl. As we drove away, I quietly prayed
for the Lord to send my daughter an "Aunt Doris"—someone who would boost her morale and take her on fun trips to
the department store, someone who would be a pal to her,
someone who could make her feel important and special.

I thank God for every "Aunt Doris" in our lives. For Charlotta it was a nice man in Georgetown who bought her a piano when he noticed her natural ability in music. For Cheralyn it was a family who had a farm on the edge of town and gave her a Shetland pony when they saw her compassion for animals. These generous gifts were wonderful, sincere expressions of love from people who had invested time in getting to know the preacher's kids. Their commitment inspired us to see all that's good in a church family.

I always marvel at the many excuses I hear around church for not getting involved. Life *is* complicated now. People are working long hours, paying bills, and caring for elderly parents. We all have huge responsibilities that occupy our minds and time. Aunt Doris had all those things too. Yet somehow she allowed the Lord to use her talents to minister to one little skinny kid. Aunt Doris never sang in the choir, played the piano, or painted gorgeous paintings for the church foyer. But she used the gifts she had. She encouraged. She loved. She baked cookies. She kept a piece of candy in her pocket. She remembered birthdays. She gave great hugs and warm kisses. *That's* talent.

Years later my brother, Mike, did me a great favor without realizing it: he married a sweet girl name Doris. My sister-in-law is now that special aunt to my children. And whenever we're together and I hear that familiar phrase roll off my children's tongues: *"Aunt Doris, can we . . . ?"* I thank God for now and for then.

Thank you, Aunt Doris.

29

RENAE
RYAN

I had a great heritage—parents who laid a solid Christian foundation. In our Mennonite community my father became a lay minister during the evening hours, a farmer and cowboy during the day. On Sundays he was a Sunday School teacher. Mom fed college kids around our table on Sundays and taught Bible studies to many of them. My parents' faith was passed along to me. So why did I experience the nagging desire for more?

September 11, 2001, was an exceptionally quiet morning for me. I didn't even turn on the television. My husband, Ron, called to give me the news of the terrorist attacks. As CEO and owner of our company (an international airline), he was in Milwaukee at a travel/airline tradeshow with Jeff, the president of our company. I was immediately concerned for the crews and passengers of the 35 flights of our airline that were still in the air. The Federal Aviation Administration had ordered all flights to be grounded immediately. Space on the ground for large aircraft was becoming a problem, so we finally diverted some planes to Canada.

After our flights were safely on the ground, I turned my attention to getting Ron and Jeff home quickly and safely. The airline needed its top executives at headquarters. With all aircraft grounded, I did all I knew to do: pray, concentrate, push, think—get them home. After many hours and prayers, we got it all arranged, and they came home. Mission accomplished.

Ron had owned the airline since 1972. He lived, breathed, and loved it. When we met and married, the airline became my love as well. We were constantly on the go with meetings, customers, and travel. Our days were full, and life was a packed suitcase.

A year ago we started thinking about selling the company. The timing was good, and Ron wanted to slow down, feeling that retirement would be a relief. But I had one nagging thought: *If we retire, who will I be? What will happen?*

Ron had always wanted to live in Florida. We finally settled in Aventura, Florida, in a great condo community close to an airport. I went to work finding the right church, the best restaurants, the closest Wal-Mart—all the things that matter most when one makes a move.

We knew that Ft. Lauderdale had some great churches, so Ron and I looked through the Yellow Pages. We saw the picture of a radiant pastor and his wife with the information of a church that was just 30 minutes from home. That is how we came to find what I now call my "passing the faith along" church.

I immediately got involved in the women's Bible study group. Our prior lives had required so much travel that I had never been able to really enjoy the benefits of sharing with other Christians on a regular basis. Our Bible study group quickly became one of the greatest benefits of our retirement.

As I headed to Bible study one Tuesday morning, I had no idea that my life was about to move in a marvelous direction. That morning God's glory fell on our group, and I will never be the same. It was what it must have been like in Num. 20:6, when the glory of the Lord filled the Temple. People couldn't wait to find out what happened in our study, and they stood outside the door. It seemed there were miracles happening every week. Women were being saved in Bible study; families were being transformed. I determined that I was going to pass my faith along to anyone who would listen.

Just a few days ago I had the opportunity to share my faith when I met two young ladies on the beach. As April, Beth, and I got acquainted, we talked about our educational training. Finally, one of them asked me, "How can you be satisfied without a career of your own?" They wondered why I hadn't taken my degree in music to a higher level. They were dismayed that my married life had been focused on working with my husband running our company. "Don't you feel cheated?"

It was a joy to share with them the satisfaction I've enjoyed since the Tuesday morning Bible study when I experienced God's glory. I began to share with April and Beth how I had become satisfied with Jesus and how He had absolutely changed my life.

I felt God's thumb in my back and boldly said, "The things that lead to dissatisfaction include pride, idolatry, low self-esteem, ego—all the 'us and me' things. There's only one way to be truly fulfilled. Only Jesus can satisfy our souls. He's the only one who can make us whole."

I was out of words, and I paused. Then the Holy Spirit took over, and I continued. "If you have an attentive husband, obedient kids, a great job, that's great. But the ultimate fulfillment is Jesus. Whatever the crisis, He's the one you must look to. Is Jesus enough regardless of your circumstances?"

I told them about my dad, whose motto for life was "Love the Lord your God with all your heart, soul, mind, and strength; then do as you please." A life focused on Jesus is a life filled with joy.

I don't know what April and Beth did with my message, but I know what sharing with them did for me. It was a blessing to pass on to them what my parents had passed on to me.

When we're satisfied with Jesus, everything else is a bonus.

30
CHLOE
SCHWEITZER

I'm not sure how I knew. I just knew. But I kept the secret buried for a long time. I didn't breathe a word to a living soul. As I became aware of it, I began to pray for my husband. The more I prayed, the more the Holy Spirit impressed upon me the certainty of what I already knew. For nearly ten years I prayed.

Then one January day my husband came home and asked for a divorce. *Did he have another woman?* I knew the answer was no. Little by little the story tumbled out, and my secret was no longer a secret. I told him I knew he was struggling with homosexuality. He was fully convinced that this lifestyle was the way for him. I wanted to work through it with him, but he moved out.

I felt betrayed and that God had forsaken me. *How could He let this happen? Did my ten years of praying mean nothing?* I prayed that God would not allow me to become bitter.

A few months later, my husband called to say that he hadn't been feeling good and had been to the doctor. The news was not good. He was suffering from a rare disease that was so new that it didn't even have a name. But he was sure he would beat it. He was strong and in excellent physical shape otherwise. He intended to pursue the divorce and go his own way.

The following July the name of the disease he suffered from was splashed across the cover of *Time*: AIDS—acquired immune deficiency syndrome. My husband was one of the first people to be diagnosed in the United States.

A year later, the divorce was granted. But my husband was anything but free. The deterioration process had begun, and for the next two years his strong body succumbed to AIDS.

But God had not forgotten my ten years of prayers. One Sunday afternoon I went to see my husband in the hospital. I pulled a chair close to the bedside. Tears began to run gently down his face as he told me of the conversation with God he had just had. He said, "I've sinned, Chloe, and I'm paying for it with my life. But today I asked God to forgive me, and He has." He continued: "I've made such a mess of our lives. Could you find it in your heart to forgive me too?"

He had one final request. He asked me to remarry him, if only in the legal sense, and help him say to the world that he had been wrong. We were remarried on Wednesday, and on Thursday he began the dying process. On Saturday he was gone. The secret was out for all to know. God had brought me through a place so dark that I thought I couldn't survive.

But I did survive, and the best was yet to come. After raising two children, finishing a career in teaching, and helping my sister care for our aging parents, God opened the door for me to teach English in Moscow, Russia. What a marvelous experience it has been!

As I reflect on the experience with my husband, several questions surface.

Did God really desert me when I felt He had forgotten to be gracious to me? No. I can see now that God was working all along.

Did my Christianity exempt me from suffering extreme emotional pain? No. But His grace helped me hang on and bear it during the darkest hours.

How did I cope with the pain that seemed unending? I really don't know. I just threw myself on the mercy of God every day.

Did my children and I suffer the consequences of my husband's decisions? Yes. Even today my children bear feelings of disappointment because of their father's sin and disobedience to God.

Did we become infected with AIDS? No. After being followed by the Center for Disease Control for two years, our blood tests showed that we were virus-free. Almost 20 years later, we all remain free of any trace of AIDS.

Has God ever told me why this happened? Not really. But He's given me peace while I wait to understand it. Until then, I'll leave it with Him.

Today I'm fighting breast cancer. After extensive surgery, I began chemotherapy. During my last treatment, the nurse told me that I was taking the very strongest chemotherapy available. The Holy Spirit seemed to whisper to me, *Chloe, when the world throws the worst at you, My grace is still sufficient.*

The most exciting news is that I'll be able to return to Russia when my treatments are completed. My faith is stronger than ever.

I'm living proof that God can keep us anywhere and put us back together after anything. What He's done for me He'll do for you.

31

KIM
SINGSON

Dense, dark smoke billowed into the sky near the intersection just ahead. Behind me I heard the sounds of bullets zinging and bombs blasting all around me. Burning houses and grenades were a way of life in war-torn Manipur, India. As I left home that morning to travel to our missionary training session in Pune, I prayed that God would protect me from the dangers I knew I would encounter. Although the perils were very real, I can honestly say that I had deep peace. Even though no one accompanied me, I knew I was not alone. My Heavenly Father was right by my side.

After my beloved husband and I completed our master's degrees and both of us were ordained, we ministered together, writing, translating, preaching, visiting, and counseling. But our joy was overshadowed when he was diagnosed with cancer. Knowing that his time was short, we talked deeply, and we agreed that the work must continue. There was no doubt that God wanted our ministry to go on. I had received such a great heritage by being brought up in a good Christian home and had shared my life with a wonderful Christian mate. I knew I had to carry my faith forward.

When I became a widow three months later, I was saddened by my enormous loss. But I knew I was never alone.

As I made my way through the strife-torn area that day, I reflected on the way the Lord had guided me when I was just ten years old. Famine had broken out in our area, and my parents became critically ill. There was no medicine to help them, and it was up to me to support my family and take care of my parents. I was able to go to school for only one-half hour that entire year. But our faith held steady, and God helped me to finally obtain medicine that immediately helped both of them begin to get well. God healed my parents completely. Although I had hardly been in class, when I took my final exams at the end of that year, I came in third. God had taken care of all of us.

I recalled another time, October 10, 2003, at 11:00 A.M. in Secunderabad, India, when God miraculously delivered a demon-possessed girl during a missionary conference. The Lord spoke distinctly to me. I acknowledged His power, and as I prayed, the demons were cast out in the name of Jesus. On May 2, 2004, God again cast out demons as I prayed. Both these girls continue to be very involved and active in their respective churches.

As I reflect back on God's healing the sick, making demons flee, and giving hope to carry on in the midst of great loss, my faith is renewed. Every time I begin to feel anxious because of troubles and hardship and not knowing if I'll live to see another day, I praise God for my heritage and His graciousness to me in the past. My anxiety immediately becomes hope, because I know that He who has called me is faithful.

Here are some thoughts I would like to pass on to my children and others to whom I minister:

- God permits us to suffer, but He never puts us to shame.
- Without faith, there's no work from God. With small faith, God works a little, but with great faith He works abundantly.
- God's work depends upon the faith we have in Him.
- Following Him is not always an easy road. It may be painful physically, but it's always joyful spiritually.
- Suffering is the significance of God's love for us.

That day as I made my way through the fire and smoke of a war zone, picking a path through the rubble, I recalled the promises in Isa. 43:1-3:

Fear not, for I have redeemed you; I have summoned you by name; you are mine. When you pass through the waters, I will be with you; and when you pass through the rivers, they will not sweep over you. When you walk through the fire, you will not be

burned; the flames will not set you ablaze. For I am the
LORD, your God, the Holy One of Israel, your Savior;

What a great comfort to know that my Savior and Re-
deemer was with me, protecting and guiding every step I
took! I traveled through a battlefield that day without getting
a scratch. With great joy and assurance, I can tell everyone
who comes after me that truly our Heavenly Father will hold
our faith steady—even in the fire.

32
CARLA
SUNBERG

I'm a missionary living in Moscow. The streets of this well-known Russian city are known for mob hits. Recently, an American journalist was gunned down right in front of his downtown office.

A few days after the journalist was killed, I was walking home from church when a big, black Volvo screeched to a halt directly in front of me. The doors swung open, and two large men jumped out. I thought for sure I was about to witness a mob hit. Just as I was looking for a place to run and hide, one of the men reached into the car and grabbed a gym bag. He briskly made his way across the street to the local fitness center. I took a deep breath as I realized that he was simply a rich Russian with a personal driver and bodyguard. I hurried on to the safety of our nearby apartment.

When I got home after that experience, I started thinking about the things I take for granted. Lately a number of things in my life have caused me to question whether I'm trusting God. Maybe it's midlife crisis, but I've been evaluating where I am in life. I've met certain goals that I felt the Lord gave me, and now I'm asking myself and Him, *What now?*

A wise friend, my Christian mentor, wrote to me and told me to live each day to the fullest and to trust Him for what He has in store for that particular day. Following that advice, I've begun to pray that God will lead me to enjoy the adventure of each and every day and to use all I've learned for whatever comes my way.

God gave me the chance to practice right away. My husband, Chuck, was supposed to lead a Work and Witness project in a town three hours west of Moscow. When the time came, he had to be away at an official church meeting, and I was left to work with the team.

One thing that has strengthened my prayer life is driving in Russia. Drivers here use sidewalks as extra lanes and dart in and out of traffic frantically. I hate driving here, but there are times I can't avoid it, and driving to the project west of Moscow was one of those times. To make matters worse, I had been running on too little sleep for days, and I was worried about staying awake for the journey, so I asked the project leader to select someone to ride with me.

The Lord sent exactly the right person to keep me company. We had a good time talking and sharing the whole time. We were an unlikely pair, but the Lord put us together for three hours, and a bond was formed. What loomed as an unwelcome task turned out to be a special day.

A few days later we were working busily at the project site with all the team members. We were doing construction work and also conducting a medical clinic, where I was working as nurse and translator for a physician visiting from the United States. Near the end of a long and tiring day, a frail woman walked into the clinic. I guessed her to be in her early 60s, but when we took her medical history we discovered she was only 38 years old. She was an alcoholic who lived with her 17-year-old daughter and 3-year-old granddaughter. We talked to her about her life and what the use of alcohol was doing to her body.

As we talked, the woman said her little granddaughter had a problem and asked if she could go get her. When we agreed, she returned a few minutes later with a beautiful but filthy little girl who had insect bites all over her legs. The bites were infected and were oozing and dripping with pus.

So this was what the Lord meant by taking each day as it comes and helping those we meet along the way.

We had no tub in which to bathe the little girl, so we lined a garbage can with a plastic bag and filled it with warm water. We stood her in the water and let her painful wounds soak. Then we dressed each wound and sent her on her way, telling the grandmother to bring her back the next day.

They returned the next day and we repeated the process. Right away we noticed a change in the grandmother. Somehow she looked younger. She had cleaned herself up and was even wearing some makeup. On the third day the grand-mother brought her daughter with her as well as her grand-daughter. Again, the little girl soaked, and we dressed her wounds. The grandmother looked even better, and she had colored her hair. The Work and Witness team sent the family home with a supply of new, clean clothing for the little girl.

On Sunday the grandmother came to church. She sat beside one of the team members, and at the end of the service they held hands and prayed together.

The other day, my new friend from the car ride E-mailed me. She said she felt the Lord wanted her to share a verse of Scripture with me and suggested I look up Ps. 37:4. "Delight yourself in the LORD and he will give you the desires of your heart."

I'm learning to delight myself in the Lord from day to day. And as I do that, I discover that He doesn't just give me the desires of my heart—He also shows me what the desires of my heart ultimately, really are. They're not necessarily the things I thought I wanted. After all, the Lord knows me better than I know myself.

As I travel through midlife, I'm working hard to trust in Him each and every day, and He's granting me the desires of my heart. He gives me a faith lift just when I need it— enough to face each day.

33
BECKY
TIRABASSI

Faith is being sure of what we hope for and certain of what we do not see (Heb. 11:1).

How do we receive the peaceful assurance from God that "all things work together for good to those who love God, to those who are the called according to His purpose" (Rom. 8:28, NKJV)? Where does this come from? How can we be sure we're not just chasing after an elusive dream, a "pot of gold" or a rainbow? And where and how does prayer enter into the process of faith—believing in what we expect to come to pass but can't physically see?

With the excitement and anticipation of a new building project, an architect and a contractor sit with an owner-buyer, assuring him or her of successful completion of the project by displaying blueprints, pictures, and sketches of similar completed buildings. They show the owner flowcharts of dates for breaking ground, erecting steel, pouring concrete, and doing finish work, detailing all the components of the building, though not even begun, but eventually to be finished and seen by all.

Similarly, time spent with God in conversation regarding dreams and hopes puts a form and plan to one's heart's desires proposing that in God's timing and by His blueprint they will come to pass. Daily discussions with God, the author and perfecter of our faith, the architect of our lives, only solidify details, develop a calm assurance, and intensify one's hope for completion of one's "building" providing "brick and mortar" for a previously "vacant lot."

Because an idea or a dream starts in one's heart and mind, faith to believe it cannot be based on outer circumstances; it must be based on God's inner work of confidence and direction—through His Word and Spirit—which will in turn provide visible "markers" as confirmation along the way.

Yet faith is not passive. It's an action, as is love. To love is to give, to accept, to sacrifice, to stand with, to believe in.

To have faith is to step in the direction toward what is believed to be the planned course of our lives. It's obeying God in the unseen areas of our lives. And because it's fueled by God alone, faith cannot develop without prayer and the

Word. It's the consecutive strings of thoughts, Scripture, and promptings heard in the inner person—*Keep moving; turn here; stop a moment; knock on this door; stop right now*—that propels us through the course of a dream, a project, or an idea.

But how can we obey if we haven't heard Him speak? Prayer and the Word whisper, call out, point, promise, and goad us in each and every step—*if* we will only take time to listen.

Faith cannot be mustered up, engineered, or manipulated; it's a response from within us, orchestrated by God. It's a supernatural confidence inspired by a supernatural God.

I often shake my head in awe at the miracle of my conversion to Christ. For six years, from age 15 to 21, I followed all the "popular" trends: going to wild parties, drinking, dancing, bar-hopping, and using drugs. I was caught in a downward spiral—going from a normal, happy, all-American kid to becoming an alcoholic drug addict with suicidal tendencies.

An unusual course of events led me to a small church with one born-again, Spirit-filled janitor on its staff who loved to share Christ with the lost. *Never* in my wildest thoughts would I have imagined my life turning 180 degrees one hot, sunny August California afternoon at the persuasion of this man.

How did he convince me to be born again when my boyfriend, lifestyle, and future looked so worldly? He spoke these words: "If anyone is in Christ, he is a new creation; old things have passed away; behold, all things have become new" (2 Cor. 5:17, NKJV). And though this janitor knew of my past and present, he told me that Jesus loved me—just the way I was!

Why by his suggestion and without struggle or reservation on my part would I ask Jesus Christ into my heart? Though I could not see ahead, looking back was so painful that the words he spoke offered me hope for a new life. My previous "religious" experiences were not the basis for that all-encompassing, daring faith. Nor had I been able to quit drinking or using drugs by my own self-determination. No, I was *without hope* for healing, with no money even for outpatient recovery. I had literally depleted any reservoir of self-respect. What could cause such a turnaround?

I believe the first step of faith took place when I believed what the janitor said about his Jesus: (1) He did and would always love me, and (2) He was going to make my life new.

The second step occurred when I repeated the "sinner's prayer," begging Jesus to come into my heart and forgive me for my many sins and make me new. I walked away from that time in prayer convinced that I was a brand-new person! There's no other explanation for why the compelling thought or drive to have a drink, that craving or physical need for alcohol, had been removed from my life, *never* to return. In that moment of prayer, I was miraculously released from the bondage alcohol had upon me. Equally drastic changes in my lifestyle, friends, and habits were just the initial wave of new life in Christ!

Almost immediately strange and unusual cravings developed within me, only hours after my conversion: to read the Bible, to pray, and to tell others about Jesus.

To say I was a former sinner who had been saved would be stating the depth of my depravity mildly. Yet the question remained: How could I have changed so abruptly and dramatically?

119

I can attribute the accelerated changes in a few short months—

from alcoholic to evangelist,
from worldly to spiritual,
from a foul mouth to a clean mouth,
from immoral to moral,
from habitual liar to truth-teller,
from worrier to pray-er,
from pagan to incessant Bible reader—

only to a faith supernaturally implanted within me to believe in the living Christ and His Word. The moment I dared to believe that Jesus could and would change my life from old to new, though I could not see how, and chose to believe God's Word as literal, I was rescued, delivered, and saved through faith in the Son of God.

Less than one month after my born-again experience, a small group of Christians laid hands on a completely sober and "straight" 21-year-old and prayed a seemingly unfit prayer. They prayed for God's Holy Spirit to empower me as an evangelist—throughout the world. Strange, huh? I had barely escaped the fires of hell, and they had me gallivanting across the world sharing about Jesus! And it would be months later before I would read 1 Tim. 4:14: "Do not neglect your gift, which was given you through a prophetic message when the body of elders laid their hands on you."

Not knowledgeable regarding Christian organizations or the church, I returned to my parents' hometown and within a year was on staff with a local Youth for Christ chapter. Over the past 13 years I've been sharing my testimony through both spoken and written media throughout the United States and in other countries.

Could I ever have imagined that in the first months after my conversion to Christ, God would have such a detailed and dynamic plan for one who was so lost? No. But faith is believing what you cannot see. It's taking a step toward where you believe God is leading. It's not looking back. It's not trying to rationalize. It's not trying to discover logical reasoning. It's daring to believe that the God of this universe can direct one's life, able and willing to intervene to bring the "dead" spiritually to life, to bring healing and health, and to give hope for tomorrow—no matter how bleak tomorrow looks.

Prayer and faith combine the appointments with the architect and the subsequent action steps that He directs in fulfilling God's purpose for one's life. Whether it's pouring the concrete of the foundation, laying just one brick in the huge process, or looking back on an addition completed, faith is the "stuff" a Christian's life can't do without. Heb. 11:6 challenges, "Without faith it is impossible to please God."

34

DONNA LEE TONEY

I had the good fortune to be born to parents who lived the faith they taught my siblings and me. While memories of fun, laughter, and living in a home filled with joy flood my mind, the underlying foundation that was laid by my parents is what anchors me as an adult living in today's sometimes-brutal world. My mother never missed the chance to nurture and instill the basics of biblical teaching in just about every setting. She lived out Deut. 6:6-7, 9:

"These commandments that I give you today are to be upon your hearts. Impress them on your children. Talk about them when you sit at home and when you walk along the road, when you lie down and when you get up. . . . Write them on the door frames of your houses and on your gates."

My folks did that, but as children we never knew that the lessons they taught were "devotionals." Nevertheless, godly principles were helping establish core values based on God's Word. Mother's ears and heart were keen on picking up the little things we said, and she knew how to draw out the conflicts we encountered every day. Many times as I stood next to her at the sink while I dried dishes, she gently probed about my day. Through conversation, she caused us kids to contemplate the meaning of others' actions, always pointing out that we should overlook another person's mistakes but learn from them rather than follow the crowd. She quipped, "You'll make plenty of your own mistakes—no need to repeat someone else's."

We were taught the art of thinking for ourselves and arriving at our own conclusions so that when asked about our faith, we had a response. Because we had thought out our own reasons for doing or not doing what our friends proposed, we could stand on our own two feet. My mother distinguished the difference between being guided and being ruled. Children who grow up without learning how to deal with peer pressure often become insecure adults who are always trying to "measure up."

Acceptance from classmates is a driving force in elementary school. Being cool at any cost is of major importance to most teenagers. Parents often allow their kids to compromise on their dress and what they listen to so they won't be outcasts. By the time that child reaches adulthood, he or she may have developed the habit of conforming to popular trends regardless of the consequences.

The desire to gain the acceptance of peers is a crowd-pleaser. But sadly, one can be trampled by a crowd. Isa. 7:9 says, "If you do not stand firm in your faith, you will not stand at all." I was privileged to have this stitched into the fabric of my raising.

It's thrilling to read the authentic biographies of those who lived out their faith—faith that produced fruit reflecting the attributes of God.

Fellowship. The Bible says that Noah was a righteous man, blameless among his people. His faith was fine-tuned through his fellowship with God. He believed God's Word so completely that he built an ark on dry land as his neighbors scoffed at him. Noah stood alone among men but was used by God to save humanity.

Action. Joseph was filled with faith in action even as a young boy who was left for dead by his jealous brothers. When he was tempted by his master's wife, he fled from her evil clutches (Gen. 39:10). Though he was wrongly accused and stripped of his status, God remembered him and showed him favor. God intervened and used Joseph to take action in order to sustain his brothers, family, and God's chosen people.

Inspiration. Moses understood the art of standing alone. As a young man he was ridiculed by his own people and pursued viciously by the royal house in which he was raised. Confronted by a burning bush, Moses stood alone in the blazing fire of God's presence. Inspired by the "ultimate fireside chat," he stood at the foot of Pharaoh's mighty throne and led a nation out of bondage. In spite of his lack of eloquent speech, by faith Moses ascended the mountain alone and was inspired in God's presence as the Author of Life wrote in stone the standard of conduct for mankind.

Trust. Job was stripped of almost everything—his wealth, his place in society, his friends, his family, even his wife. Everything but his faith. The Bible says Job was blameless and upright and was the greatest man among all the people of the East. Satan was permitted to test Job and made sure to surround him with "friends" who belabored his woes as they denounced the power of his God. As Job sat in sackcloth and ashes in the midst of utter despair, he proclaimed, "Though he slay me, yet will I trust in him" (Job 13:15, KJV). Job was tested because of his trust in God, and his trust proved that God never forsakes us, though we may seem to be alone in dire circumstances.

Holiness. Young Daniel, as he was trained in the royal court, declared that he would not defile himself by eating from the king's table. He would not eat certain foods that compromised his faith, even if offered him by the king. He would not yield to peer pressure from those who surrounded him. Daniel meant no disrespect by rejecting the fine food and drink. He simply took a higher road. In wisdom, he asked the chief official to set him apart so he would be more fit for service to the king. Daniel proved better than those who ate and drank from the table of the king. He was subsequently elevated in the kingdom and was ultimately ushered into the palace second only to the ruler of the land. His jealous rivals persuaded the king to make a decree that no one could pray to any other god except King Darius. Though Daniel heard the decree, he did not curtail his fellowship with God. His peers spied on him, caught him praying, and reported it to the king. With sorrow, the king cast Daniel into the lion's den as punishment. God miraculously shut the mouths of the king's ferocious cats. When King Darius, who had grown fond of Daniel, heard Daniel's voice and realized he had not been devoured, Daniel was lifted out of the den.

Next time your faith wavers in the face of peer pressure, notice Noah: he did not compromise his faith in the face of his mockers—he sailed. Consider Joseph: he did not compromise his faith when he was tempted—he ran! Ponder Moses: he did not compromise faith by worshipping idols—he ascended the mountain to hear from God. Contemplate Job: he did not compromise his faith by giving in to despair—he trusted. And think of Daniel: he did not compromise his faith by obeying the king's decree—he prayed. Above all, remember Christ: He did not compromise His faith by coming down from the Cross—He rose!

I remember when I was a little girl Daddy pushing back from the table after supper, picking up his guitar, and singing, *You've got to keep walking, keep walking, walking in the light of the Lord.*

Faith is not an empty word.

Forging
Ahead
I
Trust
Him.

35
CARLA VAN DER KOOIJ

*I*t was getting dark the evening Maria's mother brought her to the House of Refuge, a home I founded in Brazil for children with HIV/AIDS. Maria was like an animal, jabbering as she dashed through the door to the tropical garden in the back, where she hid under the foliage. To four-year-old Maria, being inside was like being in a cage. Mentally and emotionally disturbed, she was unable to say a word; her crossed eyes darted wildly back and forth.

I responded to God's call on my life and left Holland in 1988 to go to Brazil to work with orphans and abandoned children infected with the HIV/AIDS virus. Affiliated with Youth with a Mission, I began plans for a home for the little ones. Finally, in 1993, House of Refuge opened.

Maria had never lived a normal life. When she came to us, she was not accustomed to using a toilet and simply squatted in the center of the garden. We trained her to use the bathroom.

Maria's mother was HIV positive and felt unable to care for Maria. All four of her children were infected with the virus and lived with her in a barn. Two of Maria's siblings had already died of AIDS when she came to live with us. For Maria, the House of Refuge became a safe harbor.

Maria began to make progress, and she began to talk. One day she prayed and asked Jesus to come into her heart, and we rejoiced with her. We were saddened, though, when Maria's mother returned and took her back. That was the beginning of a pattern in which Maria would stay with us for a while and then be taken away by her mother.

It became apparent to us that Maria was being abused sexually, and she became increasingly disturbed emotionally. Her behavior deteriorated in every way. Finally, her home visits were ended, and we carefully supervised her contact with her mother.

When Maria's mother died, we tried to console her. We reminded her of the prayer she had prayed when she asked Jesus to come into her heart. As I held her close, I assured her that Jesus loved her.

That evening, all the children gathered around to pray that Jesus would be with Maria. The next morning, Maria could hardly wait to tell us that our prayers had been answered. She said, "Jesus came and stayed beside me all night. And when I woke up this morning, He was still there." The children were not surprised. They had been taught that Jesus drew little children close to His side.

In the stable environment of the House of Refuge, Maria began to settle down, and she soon blossomed. She had a beautiful singing voice and was a talented artist.

Maria was especially attached to me. When I had surgery, she was my best nurse, singing to me and drawing beautiful pictures of flowers to cheer me. When she brought my meal tray, she insisted that I eat everything on it so that I could grow stronger.

In 2001 I turned over the day-to-day operation of the House of Refuse to the Brazilian caregivers, but I'm still very much involved in training, facilitating, and caring for the children.

Watching the children develop spiritually and physically in the loving environment of the House of Refuge brings me great joy. Many of the children have been adopted, some have gone to be with Jesus, and others now live with members of their extended families. Although many of the children come to us without hope, their lives blossom in spite of the unthinkable tragedies they've experienced. Through the House of Refuge, they find comfort and joy in the midst of their sorrow and suffering.

Maria no longer lives in the dirt. She's becoming a beautiful young woman, though with the mind of a six-year-old child. She loves to sing worship songs by heart. Recent optical surgery was successful, and her eyes are no longer crossed.

By God's grace, Maria has become a reflection of her lovely paintings—a beautiful flower of blossoming hope.

36

MARJORIE MORGRIDGE WENIGER

Years ago, I worked as a door-to-door saleswoman. I didn't even like knocking on doors, but I believed in my product, so I persevered. My perseverance paid off in an unexpected way when I met Eva, a gentle, loving person. One day she and I began to talk about our faith, and I told her my faith needed to be stronger. She encouraged me to participate in a Bible study she was involved in. I agreed to begin a study in my home, and I invited my friends and neighbors. It was a turning point in my life.

A few months later, I knelt by my bed and prayed, *Jesus, I know I'm a sinner. I ask you to forgive me. You died on the Cross for me. I invite you to come into my heart and be my Savior.*

Life took on new meaning for me. I began to devour God's Word. I desired to become a woman of prayer, and I wanted to learn to share my faith with others. Other ladies in our study also accepted Jesus and became leaders in their churches. Some began hosting Bible studies.

I often think about the way God used Eva to lead me to faith, and I used studies in my home to reach out to others. Then God opened the door for me to present "Reach Out," a radio mentoring program I've hosted for years.

Shortly after my first husband's death, my church asked me to begin a mentoring program through which older ladies could invest their time, prayers, and experience in the lives of younger women. I accepted the challenge, and the Titus Two ministry was born. We based it on Titus 2:3-5:

> Teach the older women to be reverent in the way they live, not to be slanderers or addicted to much wine, but to teach what is good. Then they can train the younger women to love their husbands and children, to be self-controlled and pure, to be busy at home, to be kind, and to be subject to their husbands, so that no one will malign the word of God.

Younger women still need role models and mentors today. I thank God for Eva and others who invested in my life, and I'm committed to passing on my faith by mentoring the next generation.

Like a pebble tossed into a large pool, the ripples are far-reaching. My prayer is that I may keep tossing pebbles of faith into the lives of those around me.

37

KACI
WILLIAMS

I've had it good. I grew up in a Christian home, and I've been involved in youth ministries and church groups. And even though I was often given the opportunity to share my testimony with several groups, I was always reluctant. I thought my story was bland. I had never experienced a life-change trauma or a turn-around point, so I thought my story wouldn't be powerful. I thought my friends who were saved later in life had more dramatic stories to share.

My Bible study teacher pointed out to me that a Christian who continues to love the Lord from an early age can be a powerful witness to the unending, never-changing love of Jesus Christ. The testimony of a lifelong Christian proves that when God begins a good work, He carries it out until the end.

This got me to thinking about my faith. Growing up, I knew there was something wonderfully different about my family. My brothers and I didn't always get along, but we shared an underlying love that was the foundation on which we now build our friendships. My parents loved each other, and the only discipline I ever needed was to hear my full name in my father's strong, stern voice. I have always been close with my extended family, and my cousins became great friends. My cousin Molly is my best friend.

A major influence in my life growing up was Kanakuk, a Christian athletic summer camp in southwestern Missouri. When I was a child, I learned from counselors and staff just what living for the Lord looks like. When I got older, it was my turn to fill the shoes of counselor and pass on my faith to the young campers under my care.

The first summer I served as a camp counselor I worked alongside Molly, my brothers, and other cousins and close friends. I had my own cabin full of little girls to disciple and play with all day long. I learned that while I was pouring myself into these girls, teaching them, helping them, loving them, even just making sure they got from one place to the next during the day, I was running out of strength. I soon realized the importance of nurturing myself with God's Word.

There were hundreds of other college-aged Christians working there who were just as excited as I was. But the encouragement of fellow staff and my family was not enough sometimes. The best place to draw strength was from the Lord. My quiet time and prayer time became an essential part of my day.

It was hard to say goodbye to my campers when it was time for them to go. I had to trust the Lord to help me move on, and I knew His hand would be on these girls as they went back to their everyday lives.

As that summer's camp drew to a close, Molly and I decided to embark on another endeavor and become counselors at an unusual camp. Camp Barnabas was different from Kanakuk in that it hosted physically and mentally handicapped children. The week we spent at Camp Barnabas took us outside our comfort zones.

Each counselor was assigned to one camper due to the level of care each camper required. Many of them needed assistance dressing, using the bathroom, bathing, and even eating. Several campers couldn't speak or communicate clearly. This was quite a change from Kanakuk, but we knew the Lord would provide us the strength we needed.

I spent hours each day playing in the dirt, because that's what my camper liked to do. Molly's camper needed constant movement, so they walked and spent hours swinging. When our campers became frustrated in group activities and wandered into quieter areas, all we could do was follow and watch over them the best we could. Although each day we grew more weary and longed for a normal conversation with someone, the Lord was faithful and helped us through.

In the end, it proved to be the most faith-building week of my life. I was forced to rely completely on God, and He gave me everything I needed to impact the life of my camper.

Molly and I will never forget our time at Kanakuk and Barnabas. We both learned that the faith we were given from our parents can't be kept to ourselves. Sharing ourselves with our campers and fellow counselors was so rewarding that we've been inspired to continue sharing our faith and lives even now that camp is over.

I'm determined to do more than just keep the faith—I plan to spread it!

38
YESODAMMA

Pastor Solomon Dinakaran and his wife, Selvi Mary, pastor a church in Whitefield, India, that sponsors a tailoring school. Yesodamma was accepted by the tailoring school, and on her first day of training she eagerly hurried to the church to begin her classes. Somehow she knew that her life would be changed forever because of the new things she was about to learn.

Day after day, Yesodamma attended classes, and the teachers patiently taught the basics of tailoring and operating the old treadle sewing machines. Before long, Yesodamma had learned the rhythm and coordination required to guide the soft, silky fabric with her hands as she pumped the treadle with her feet. With awe, she smoothed the first colorful scarf she sewed. She knew she would enjoy tailoring for the rest of her life.

But tailoring wasn't the only thing she learned. Every day the ladies took a break from sewing classes. Pastor Solomon and Selvi taught them about Jesus. Yesodamma had heard the name of Jesus, but she didn't know His story. She listened intently as Solomon and Selvi taught from the Bible. After Bible study one day, Yesodamma went back to her sewing machine, but she watched through the open classroom door as two ladies who had lingered behind knelt to pray. As her feet moved back and forth and her hands guided the fabric, Yesodamma pondered what she had seen.

After several months, Yesodamma's sewing classes were completed. She beamed with joy as she received her certificate with the rest of her graduating class.

When she returned to her village that evening, a friend told her about a factory that had an opening for a tailor. Early the next morning, clutching her brand new certificate, she hurried to the factory. She was immediately given a job. Her life and that of her family were changed drastically for the better by this new source of income.

As Yesodamma sewed day after day in the factory, she often thought about those Bible studies she had attended. A deep hunger began to grow within her. Although she found satisfaction in providing a new home and other material things for her family, there was still an emptiness inside her that had not been satisfied.

One evening a friend from her village who had been trained with Yesodamma came by to see her new home. She asked Yesodamma if she had heard about the *JESUS* film. Yesodamma had not heard of it, but she wanted to know more about Jesus. When her friend said the film would be shown in their village in two nights, Yesodamma knew that she would be there.

On the appointed night, as twilight fell, more than 150 villagers gathered in the street in the center of town. Yesodamma and her family sat on the front row. As the images flickered across the screen, Yesodamma's fatigue from a day bent over her sewing machine began to fade. She was captivated by the message that unfolded. Once again, she heard that Jesus provides peace and real happiness to those who believe in Him. At the end of the film, Yesodamma came forward. She begged the team members, "Please give this Jesus to me so that I may find the real peace and happiness that I've never known." As they knelt to pray with her, old things passed away, and all became new.

Yesodamma went home that night and threw out her idols and all the other trappings of her old religion. For the first time in her life, she fell asleep knowing the real meaning of peace.

The next evening, the follow-up team went to Yesodamma's home and gave her a copy of the New Testament in her own language. She invited the pastors to come into her home every week to hold services so that a church could be started in her village.

Because of Yesodamma's testimony and witness to her friends and relatives, the team was given permission to show the *JESUS* film in other villages. As a result, many have come to know Jesus, and the gospel has spread throughout the area. As Pastor Dinakaran says, "Families reaching families is quicker than any other method."

Now, as her fingers fly and her feet pedal, Yesodamma radiates joy and peace. She fills her little corner of the factory with a glowing testimony of Jesus' love. She still enjoys sewing and creating beautiful silk creations. But her greatest joy comes from sharing the good news of Jesus with those around her.

39

JOYCE
WILLIAMS

We have an emergency!" The flight attendant's tense, urgent whisper grabbed my attention as she leaned over my seat in the exit row. My mind began to race. We were only 15 minutes from landing at the airport in Roanoke, Virginia, my hometown. It had been a great morning—very uneventful. What was happening?

The pretty young attendant was saying, "Remember when we started this flight I asked you if you were comfortable being seated in this row? Are you familiar with the evacuation process in the event of an emergency landing? I need to make sure you're absolutely certain."

The situation seemed surreal. I began to realize that the lives of the 30-plus passengers on that small jet might be in my hands. Quickly, I answered, "That's OK. I believe I can do whatever I need to do." I pulled out the card in the seat back in front of me and reviewed the procedures intently.

The pilot's voice filled the cabin. "We have an emergency. The flaps are not working, and we are diverting this flight to Dulles International Airport, near Washington. The mountains and shorter runway make attempting to land in Roanoke too risky. We hope to be on the ground in about 15 minutes."

The passengers looked at each other. Our day had become, at best, complicated. We knew that touchdown might end far differently than we had anticipated.

The crew was wonderful, and the pilot tried to reassure us. "Don't be alarmed when you see the fire trucks and other emergency vehicles on the ground," he said. "This is routine procedure."

I confess I was uneasy. But one of the first things that came to mind was *Is it possible that in a few minutes I might see Jesus face to face? I might get to see Mama and Daddy!* They had been in heaven for many years, and I had looked forward to being reunited with them. I began to be a little excited about the possibilities. *Is this the day?*

I asked the Lord, *Do you have a special lesson to teach me?* And He began to whisper to my heart, *You are potentially the connecting link for all the passengers on this plane—the doorkeeper of the way to safety and life.*

He reminded me, *From an eternal perspective, all Christians are gatekeepers to life everlasting. Every Christian is seated on the exit row of the lives of every person he or she comes in contact with. You are the channels through which I have chosen to spread the Good News.*

As we descended toward the treetops, the pilot came back on the intercom. "We're going in. I want to warn you that we'll be approaching very fast, and the landing could be bumpy. Please be assured that we're taking all possible precautions to get you on the ground safely."

Glancing once again at the exit door, I braced for landing. The blinking lights of the emergency vehicles lined both sides of the runway, beckoning us as the plane roared toward landing. Those last few seconds seemed like minutes. When the wheels touched down, the plane raced across the runway. The pilot finally braked to a stop, and there was a collective sigh of relief as we taxied to the gate. We were instructed to collect our baggage and wait for a chartered bus to take us to Roanoke. We chattered nervously. A special bond had been formed among us in that shared airspace.

The four-hour bus ride to Roanoke was quite interesting. As I listened to my fellow passengers, I realized that a brush with death has a way of changing perspectives.

I'm so thankful that God gave me the grace to reflect on His amazing and sustaining love that held me steady during those tense moments. I'm more determined than ever to pass my faith to everyone around me. Because it really is true—I'm seated in the exit row of the lives of everyone I encounter.

Lord, help me never to miss an opportunity to point others to the way of escape you've provided for us.

FIND PEACE WITH GOD

Are you looking for peace? Ask Him to come into your heart today and forgive your sins.

P The **P**roblem is sin (Rom. 3:23).

E **E**veryone has a choice (Rom 6:23).

A God's love is **A**wesome (John 3:16).

C **C**onfession brings forgiveness (1 John 1:9).

E Jesus **E**nters your heart when you invite Him in (Rev. 3:20).

Prayer of Repentance

Dear Jesus, thank you for loving me and for dying on the Cross for me. I'm sorry for my sins. I ask you to forgive me and come into my heart. Please give me a new life and make me part of your family.

I accept you as my Lord and Savior. Thank you for your forgiveness and for the peace you give me. In your holy name I pray. Amen.

ABOUT THE CONTRIBUTORS

Lori Beckler and her husband, Bob, are cofounders of Heritage Keepers, a women's ministry dedicated to assisting women in their spiritual growth. Lori is an author and speaker. She and Bob are the parents of two grown children.

Rina Biswas is a public health nurse in Dhaka, Bangladesh. Her husband is the district superintendent of Nazarene ministries in Bangladesh.

Caroline Bruce is a student at Stanford University. She represented the United States in the 2004 Summer Olympics in Athens, Greece. She lives in Stanford, California.

Gracia Burnham and her husband, Martin, served as missionaries in the Philippines for 17 years. They were kidnapped and held captive for more than a year. Martin was killed during the rescue. Gracia is a gifted speaker and author. She and her children live in Rose Hill, Kansas.

Laura Bush is dedicated to advancing education in the United States. She supports the work of her husband, President George W. Bush, in making sure no child is left behind in school or in life. Mrs. Bush has created a national initiative, Ready to Read, Ready to Learn. She holds a master's degree in library science and is a former public school librarian. She and the president are the parents of twin daughters who are named for their grandmothers.

Marge Caldwell is an author, speaker, radio personality, and teacher of modeling and charm. She and her husband, Charles, are the parents of two children and live in Houston.

Tara Dawn Christensen, a former Miss America, is an acclaimed speaker and singer. She travels internationally encouraging women to develop self-esteem and emphasizing the importance of sexual abstinence before marriage. She and her husband, Jon, live in Tennessee.

Marty Cobb and her husband, Brent, have served as pastors and missionaries for 38 years. They have served in South Korea and the Philippines. Marty is a registered nurse and currently is studying to become a hospital chaplain. The Cobbs live in the Philippines and are the parents of three adult children.

Janet Davis recently graduated from Trevecca Nazarene University and will soon begin graduate studies. She has two sons and is looking forward to the arrival of her first grandchild. She lives in Antioch, Tennessee.

Millie Dienert is an author, Bible study teacher, and internationally known speaker. She was named "1990 American Churchwoman of the Year" by Religious Heritage of America. She and her late husband, Fred, worked with the Billy Graham Evangelistic Association. She resides in Blue Bell, Pennsylvania.

Judy Douglass is a graduate of the University of Texas with a degree in journalism. She currently assists her husband, Steve, who serves as president of Campus Crusade for Christ International. Judy and Steve are the parents of three children and reside in Orlando, Florida.

Karla Downing is the author of *Ten Lifesaving Principles for Women in Difficult Marriages* and *When Loves Hurts.* She serves in ministry to women as a group leader, speaker, and mentor. She and her husband, Monte, are the parents of three daughters and live in Yorba Linda, California.

Allyson Felix competed in the 2004 Summer Olympics in Athens, Greece. A pastor's daughter, Allyson says her greatest desire is to share her deep Christian faith with others. She lives in Sun Valley, California.

Kaitlin Fillipi, a budding writer, is a junior high school student. She enjoys her life as a preacher's daughter and lives with her family in Salina, Kansas.

Blanche Gressett is a gifted artist and teacher. She has directed women's ministries for more than 12 years throughout the state of

New York and has been involved in international missions for many years. She and her husband, George, are the parents of four children. They live in Poinciana, Florida.

Bethany Hamilton, a champion surfer, lost her left arm in a shark attack when she was 14 years old. Her unwavering faith in God is a testimony to the world of His goodness. Bethany lives with her family in Princeville, Hawaii.

Judy Hegstrom and her husband, Paul, founded LifeSkills International, a ministry dedicated to helping men, women, and children change destructive patterns and behaviors. The Hegstroms are the parents of three children and live in Aurora, Colorado.

Liz Curtis Higgs is an internationally known author and speaker. She is the author of more than 20 books. She and her husband, Bill, are the parents of two children and reside in Louisville, Kentucky.

Hope Hinson is a university student in Nashville. She has accepted God's call to develop studies in purity for youth. She presents seminars on modesty, sexual integrity, intimacy, accountability, and self-identity. She is the author of *So Much More.* Hope lives in Woodbury, Georgia.

Shirley Horner is president of Aloette Cosmetics in northern Indiana. Her husband, Neil, is a pastor. Shirley's life as a ministry mate, corporate executive, and cancer survivor gives her much to share. Shirley and Neil are the parents of two children and live in Chesterton, Indiana.

Barbara Johnson is a popular author, speaker, and humorist who has helped countless women find joy in their lives. She is often referred to as "the queen of encouragement," with more than seven million copies of her books currently in print. Barbara lives in La Habra, California.

Anne Graham Lotz carries the gospel of Jesus Christ throughout the world. The daughter of Billy and Ruth Bell Graham, Anne is the founder of AnGel Ministries, a nonprofit organization based in Raleigh, North Carolina, and is the author of numerous books. She and her husband, Dan, are the parents of three children and live in Raleigh.

Henrietta Mears was a mentor to thousands, including Bill and Vonette Bright, Billy Graham, and many entertainment professionals and business leaders. She established a retreat center in the San Bernardino Mountains of California, and many visitors there came to know Christ as a result of her ministry.

Mother Teresa was born in Albania. At the age of 12 she felt God's call to share the love of Christ as a missionary. In 1950 she started her own order, The Missionaries of Charity, devoted to caring for the poorest of the poor. She received many awards, including the Nobel Peace Prize.

Janet Museveni is the first lady of the Republic of Uganda. She is a woman of great faith and has been called one of the most influential Christian women in the world. Her platform of sexual abstinence outside of marriage is believed to be a key factor in the decrease of the spread of HIV/AIDS in Uganda. Her husband, Yoweri Museveni, was elected president of Uganda in 1986.

Lauren Ochs is a recent graduate of MidAmerica Nazarene University in Olathe, Kansas. She currently attends Kanakuk Institute in Branson, Missouri.

Melody Padgett is living a transformed life. She attends church regularly and is part of an ongoing Bible study. She has three children and lives in Amarillo, Texas.

Chonda Pierce has lived a life marked with humor, heartache, and hope. From her early memories of growing up as a preacher's kid to appearing center stage at the Grand Old Opry, she has found her unique place in life. Chondra and her husband, David, are the parents of two children and live in Nashville.

Renae Ryan is an accomplished pianist, philanthropist, and businesswoman. She and her husband, Ron, are involved in the aviation industry and in their community. The Ryans live in Aventura, Florida.

Chloe Schweitzer is a retired schoolteacher. She spent a number of years in Russia working as a volunteer teacher. A cancer survivor, Chloe loves sharing her faith and encouraging others. She has two grown children and lives in Miami, Florida.

Kim Singson is the coordinator of 17 churches throughout the Manipur area of India. She is a *JESUS* film coach and a church planter. She is the mother of three children and lives in Churachandpur, India.

Carla Sunberg and her husband, Chuck, have been missionaries to the former Soviet Union since 1992. Carla serves as director of theological education for the Church of the Nazarene in the former Soviet Union and is an ordained elder in the denomination. Carla and Chuck are the parents of two daughters and live in Moscow.

Becky Tirabassi is founder of Change Your Life, an inspirational and motivational speaking and writing ministry. She is a prolific author and speaks around the world. She and her husband, Roger, are the parents of one son and live in Newport Beach, California.

Donna Lee Toney has traveled extensively both personally and in connection with her work with Franklin Graham at Samaritan's Purse and the Billy Graham Evangelistic Association. As executive assistant and liaison for Franklin Graham, she has developed lasting friendships around the world. Donna's family is scattered across Georgia, Virginia, and Michigan. She lives in Boone, North Carolina.

Carla van der Kooij has served in several locations with Youth with a Mission. She specializes in HIV/AIDS training. Carla presently teaches and ministers in India.

Marjorie Morgridge Weniger is a gifted speaker and author. She serves as regional administrator for Stonecroft Ministries and is the coordinator of Women's Week each summer near Branson, Missouri. She has hosted "Reach Out," a daily radio ministry for more than 25 years. Several years ago Marjorie initiated a mentoring ministry that pairs young mothers with older women. She and her husband, Paul, live in Wichita, Kansas.

Kaci Williams is a student at Kansas State University in Manhattan, Kansas, where she is a member of the varsity rowing team. During summer break she works as a counselor at Kamp Kanakuk near Branson, Missouri. She is a young woman of extraordinary courage and a very dear granddaughter of the compiler. When not in school or working as a camp counselor, she makes her home with her parents and two brothers in Olathe, Kansas.